Moral Education in sub-Saharan Africa

The term 'moral' has had a chequered history in sub-Saharan Africa, mainly due to the legacy of colonialism and Apartheid (in South Africa). In contrast to moral education as a vehicle of cultural imperialism and social control, this volume shows moral education to be concerned with both private and public morality, with communal and national relationships between human beings, as well as between people and their environment. Drawing on distinctive perspectives from philosophy, economics, sociology and education, it offers the African ethic of *Ubuntu/Botho* as a plausible alternative to Western approaches to morality and shows how African ethics speaks to political and economic life, including ethnic conflict and HIV/AIDS, and may be an antidote to the current practice of timocracy that values money over people.

The volume provides sociological tools for understanding the lived morality of those marginalised by poverty, and analyses the effects of culture, religion and modern secularisation on moral education. With contributions from fourteen African scholars, this book challenges dominant frameworks, and begins conversations for mutual benefit across the North-South divide. It has global implications, not just, but especially, where moral education is undertaken in pluralist contexts and in the presence of economic disparity.

This book was published as a special issue of the *Journal of Moral Education*.

Sharlene Swartz is a sociologist and senior research specialist at the Human Sciences Research Council in South Africa, and a visiting research fellow at the University of Cambridge. She holds a masters degree from Harvard University and a PhD in the sociology of education from the University of Cambridge.

Monica Taylor is a philosopher who has worked in a national educational research organisation in the UK and has edited the *Journal of Moral Education* for 35 years. She is currently a research associate at the Institute of Education, University of London and the President of the Asia Pacific Network for Moral Education.

Moral Education in sub-Saharan Africa
Culture, Economics, Conflict and AIDS

Edited by
Sharlene Swartz and Monica Taylor

Routledge
Taylor & Francis Group

LONDON AND NEW YORK

First published 2011
by Routledge
2 Park Square, Milton Park, Abingdon, Oxon, OX14 4RN

Simultaneously published in the USA and Canada
by Routledge
711 Third Avenue, New York, NY 10017

Routledge is an imprint of the Taylor & Francis Group, an informa business

This book is a reproduction of the *Journal of Moral Education*, vol. 39, issue 3. The Publisher requests to those authors who may be citing this book to state, also, the bibliographical details of the special issue on which the book was based.

Typeset in Baskerville by Taylor & Francis Books

British Library Cataloguing in Publication Data
A catalogue record for this book is available from the British Library

ISBN 13: 978-0-415-61340-8

Disclaimer
The publisher would like to make readers aware that the chapters in this book are referred to as articles as they had been in the special issue. The publisher accepts responsibility for any inconsistencies that may have arisen in the course of preparing this volume for print.

Contents

CONTENTS

NOTES ON CONTRIBUTORS

Julia DeKadt (South Africa) is a doctoral student and a researcher at the Birth to Twenty Research Programme at the University of the Witwatersrand in South Africa. She holds a BSc in cognitive science from the Massachusetts Institute of Technology, USA, and an MA in politics and public affairs from Princeton University, USA. Her research interests lie in the implications of policy, particularly in education, for children and youth. Her PhD thesis, nearing completion at the University of the Witwatersrand, investigates learner mobility and school choice in Soweto, South Africa.

Joseph B. R. Gaie (Botswana), PhD, is a senior lecturer in philosophy at the University of Botswana where he teaches applied ethics. He graduated from the University of Essex (PhD) and Edinburgh (MSc), UK. He is interested in indigenising ethics, hence his co-editorship of a book on *The concept of Botho and HIV/AIDS in Botswana* (Zapf Chancery, Kenya, 2007) and several articles on the application of *Botho* to moral situations. He is the author of *The medical involvement in capital punishment: a philosophical discussion* (Kluwer, 2004). He is currently working on the application of *Botho/Ubuntu* to epistemology and metaphysics.

Susan Kiragu (Kenya), PhD, is a social scientist and a research associate at the Centre for Commonwealth Education, Faculty of Education, University of Cambridge, UK. She has undergraduate and masters degree in education from Kenyan universities and a masters degree and a PhD in education from the University of Cambridge. Her research interests are centred in Africa—especially on HIV/AIDS prevention, behaviour change, gender, education for social justice, the use of indigenous knowledge for teacher training and curriculum development and participatory research. She has published in journals such as *Pastoral Care in Education* and *Sex Education*, in addition to a number of book chapters.

Tawanda Makusha (Zimbabwe) is a doctoral student and research intern in the HIV, AIDS, STI and TB research programme at the Human Sciences Research Council in South Africa. He has a BA (Hons) in history and development studies from Midlands State University, Zimbabwe and an MA in development studies from the University of KwaZulu-Natal, South Africa. His PhD studies at the University of KwaZulu-Natal focus on children, men and families in the context of HIV/AIDS and poverty.

Yonah H. Matemba (Malawi) is a doctoral student at the University of Glasgow, Scotland, UK, where he also teaches on the MA religious and philosophical education teacher programme. He holds a certificate in education from Solusi University, Zimbabwe, a bachelor's degree in education from Andrews University (USA) and postgraduate degrees in history and theology from the universities of Botswana and Malawi, respectively. Previously, he has been a lecturer in religious education at Molepolole College of Education, Botswana and later at the Catholic University of Malawi. Some of his papers have appeared in journals such as *Religious Education* (USA) and the *British Journal of Religious Education.*

Thaddeus Metz (South Africa), PhD, is Research Professor in the Department of Philosophy at the University of Johannesburg, South Africa. He has a BA in philosophy and sociology from the University of Iowa and holds an MA and a PhD in philosophy from Cornell University, USA. Much of his research in ethics interprets the African morality of *ubuntu* in an analytic, rigorous way; uses a principle of respect for human dignity to resolve practical controversies; and systematically develops and evaluates theoretical approaches to what makes a life meaningful. Among his many publications are Human dignity, capital punishment, and an African moral theory: toward a new philosophy of human rights, *Journal of Human Rights,* 9(1), (2010): 81-99, and African and Western moral theories in a bioethical context, *Developing World Bioethics,* 10(1), (2010): 49-58.

Mussa K. Mohamed (Tanzania) is a science and health education facilitator at Aga Khan University, Institute of Educational Development (IED) East Africa, in Dar es Salaam, Tanzania. He has an undergraduate degree in science with education from Dar es Salaam University and holds a masters degree from Aga Khan University, IED, Pakistan. His research interests focus on improving the teaching and learning of HIV/AIDS and on promoting science literacy.

Mary Oluga (Kenya) is a lecturer in teacher education at the Aga Khan University, Institute for Educational Development East Africa (IED-EA) in Dar es Salaam, Tanzania. She holds a masters degree in teacher education from Aga Khan University, IED-EA, has a bachelor of education and a diploma in education from Kenyatta University and a certificate in teacher education from Siriba Teachers College, Kenya. She also holds a certificate in teaching and the AIDS pandemic from the University of the Western Cape, South Africa and is currently completing a PhD in curriculum development at Kenyatta University. Her research interests are in health education, the impact of HIV/AIDS on education, social studies and teacher professional development.

Mogobe B. Ramose (South Africa), PhD, is professor of philosophy at the University of South Africa. He obtained a doctor of philosophy degree from the University of Louvain (KUL) in Belgium and a master of science (International Relations) from the London School of Economics, University of London, UK. *African philosophy through Ubuntu* (Harare, Mond Books, 1999) is among his numerous publications, which also include, 'I doubt, therefore African philosophy exists' in the *South African Journal of Philosophy*, 22(2), 113–127; and seven contributions to *The African philosophy reader* edited by P.H. Coetzee and A.P.J. Roux (London, Routledge,

1998). His current interests include African philosophy and the philosophy of liberation.

Linda Richter (South Africa), PhD, is distinguished research fellow in the HIV, AIDS, STIs and TB research programme at the Human Sciences Research Council, South Africa. She holds honorary professorships at the University of KwaZulu-Natal and the University of the Witwatersrand, South Africa. She is an honorary research associate in the Department of Psychiatry at the University of Oxford, UK and a visiting scholar in the School of Public Health at Harvard University, USA. Linda publishes widely in the fields of child, adolescent and family development, infant and child assessment, protein-energy malnutrition, street and working children and the effects of HIV/AIDS on children and families, including HIV prevention among young people. Among her many publications are: *Baba: men and fatherhood in South Africa* (Cape Town, HSRC Press, 2006); *Mandela's children: growing up in post-Apartheid South Africa* (London, Routledge, 2001); and *Sexual abuse of young children in Southern Africa* (Cape Town, HSRC Press 2005).

Herménégilde Rwantabagu (Burundi), PhD, is professor of comparative international education at the University of Burundi. He holds a bachelor's degree in education from the University of East Africa (Kenya), a master's degree and a doctorate in Comparative International Education from the Institute of Education, University of London, UK, as well as a diploma in peace studies from Uppsala University, Sweden. His areas of special interest are teacher education, peace education and moral education in sub-Saharan Africa.

Sharlene Swartz (South Africa), PhD, is a sociologist and senior research specialist in the Human and Social Development research programme at the Human Sciences Research Council, South Africa. She is also visiting research fellow at the Centre for Commonwealth Education, University of Cambridge, UK. She has undergraduate degrees in science (University of the Witwatersrand) and theology (University of Zululand), both in South Africa, and holds a masters degree from Harvard University (USA) and a PhD in the sociology of education from the University of Cambridge, UK. Her research interests focus on youth and poverty, social inequality, the sociology of morality and masculinities. She is the author of *Teenage tata: voices of young fathers in South Africa* (Cape Town, HSRC Press, 2009) and *Ikasi: the moral ecology of South Africa's township youth* (New York, Palgrave Macmillan, 2009; Johannesburg, Wits Press, 2010).

Shelina Walli (Tanzania) is assistant lecturer at Aga Khan University, Institute of Educational Development East Africa (AKU IED-EA), based in Dar es Salaam, Tanzania. She has an undergraduate degree in early childhood education and a masters of education (teacher education) from AKU IED-EA. Her master's thesis considered the integration of HIV/AIDS education into the pre-school curriculum. She has a passion for early childhood and has been in the field of education in various capacities for 20 years.

Gail Weldon (South Africa), PhD, is an historian, educator and a senior curriculum Planner at the Western Cape Department of Education in Cape Town, South Africa. She has an advanced professional diploma in educational development from Leeds

Metropolitan University, UK. She holds a masters degree in history and a PhD in education policy and management studies from South African universities. She has been involved in national curriculum development processes in post-Apartheid South Africa and her research interests centre on memory, identity and curriculum in post-conflict societies.

Acknowledgements

The editors would like to thank the following, who have acted as referees for each of the papers considered for publication in this edition: Valerie Anderson, Department of Sociology, University of Cape Town, South Africa; Dr Jeremiah Chikovore, HIV, AIDS, STIs and TB research programme, Human Sciences Research Council, South Africa; Admire Chirowodza, Child, Youth, Family and Social Development research programme, Human Sciences Research Council, South Africa; Professor Rhett Diessner, Department of Psychology, Lewis-Clarke State College, USA; Dr Petro DuPreez, Faculty of Educational Sciences, North West University, South Africa; Professor Penny Enslin, Faculty of Education, University of Glasgow, Scotland, UK; Dr Joseph Gaie, Department of Theology, University of Botswana, Botswana; Professor Brian Gates, Division of Theology and Philosophy, St Martin's College, UK; Dr Patrick Giddy, School of Philosophy and Ethics, University of KwaZulu-Natal, South Africa; Professor Michael Glassman, Department of Human Development and Family Sciences, The Ohio State University, USA; Professor Jonathan Jansen, Vice Chancellor, University of the Free State, South Africa; Professor Ken Jubber, Department of Sociology, University of Cape Town, South Africa; Dr Colleen McLaughlin, Faculty of Education, University of Cambridge, UK; Professor Thaddeus Metz, Department of Philosophy, University of Johannesburg, South Africa; Dr Sana Mmolai, Department of Languages and Social Sciences Education, Faculty of Education, University of Botswana, Botswana; Dr Zitha Mokomane, Population Health, Health Systems and Innovation research programme, Human Sciences Research Council, South Africa; Dr Munyaradzi Murove, Department of Philosophy, University of KwaZulu-Natal, South Africa; Professor Jan Nieuwenhuis, Faculty of Education, University of Pretoria, South Africa; Professor Crain Soudien, Faculty of Education, University of Cape Town, South Africa; Ingrid Van Der Heijden, Department of Anthropology, Rhodes University, South Africa.

Introduction

The pain and the promise of moral education in sub-Saharan Africa

Sharlene Swartz
Human Sciences Research Council, South Africa

The term 'moral' has had a chequered history in sub-Saharan Africa, mainly due to the legacy of colonialism in Africa, and the history of Apartheid oppression in South Africa. When Apartheid's racist policies were entrenched, through a series of legislative acts beginning in 1948, the Nationalist government notoriously enacted a statute known as *The Immorality Act* (Republic of South Africa, Parliament, 1950). Sadly, the act had nothing to do with morality as we understand it today. It did not deal with kindness, human flourishing or the good life, or with the inhumane ways in which people deal with each other, or with the censure of people who perpetrate violence or perpetuate injustice. Rather this notorious *Immorality Act*, prohibited sexual intercourse and marriage between people of different 'races'. It not only served to entrench Apartheid as 'one of the great evils of the modern era' (Crais, 2002, p. 4) and 'a crime against humanity' (Truth and Reconciliation Commission, 1999, p. 94), but also forever tainted the term 'morality' by loading it with references to miscegenation, white supremacy and social control.

Furthermore, the philosophy underpinning African colonisation was largely supported by the view that colonisation was a vehicle towards the 'civilisation' of the continent, with 'civilisation' being 'not just a marker of material improvement, but also a normative judgment about the moral progress of society' (Stanford Encyclopaedia of Philosophy, 2006). Moreover 'colonising', 'civilising', 'Christianising' and 'moralising' were inextricably linked. In contrast, when renowned author, Antjie Krog speaks of 'three centuries of fractured morality' (1999, p. 68), she is referring to the immoral history of colonisation, slavery, land dispossession, conquest, subjugation and inequality in sub-Saharan Africa. 'Morality' clearly means different things to different people, and in Africa it is an especially problematic term, not least when, as is currently the case in Uganda, Malawi and Zimbabwe, sexual orientation is cause for moral censure and legal conviction.

Moral education is subsequently tainted by association, especially since it, too, has been used as a vehicle of cultural imperialism, nationalist propaganda and social (and sexual) control. Consequently, when one speaks of morality and moral education in sub-Saharan Africa as a progressive and democratic pursuit, much prior explanation is needed.

To be clear, moral education in Africa, and elsewhere, ought to be concerned with both private and public morality; with what it means to be a good person and to lead a good life. It covers intimate, communal and national relationships between human beings, as well as between people and their environment. It should be concerned with violence and crime, conflict and peace, slavery and human trafficking, social spending and consumption, judgement and incarceration, inequality and greed. It must be interested in the moral significance of social class, poverty and unemployment, as well as the moral implications of lack of housing, welfare, access to education, gender equality, freedom of opportunity, fairness, racism, homophobia, human rights and justice in all its forms. These are all moral issues, and of importance for moral education in sub-Saharan Africa.

The key question that this volume seeks to address is: what contribution can scholars from Africa concerned with moral education contribute to the multiple issues of culture, conflict, economics and HIV/AIDS that, while not peculiar to sub-Saharan Africa, are certainly acute in this region of the world? Furthermore, are there ways in which this work, frequently undertaken in difficult circumstances, can challenge prevailing and dominant Global North frameworks, and begin conversations for mutual benefit across the North South divide? The themes covered in this volume deal with much which is painful, although some promising pathways are suggested.

The promise of *Ubuntu*, moral capital and moral education

In this volume, four chapters showcase the promise of doing moral education in sub-Saharan Africa. Each offers a distinctive perspective drawn from philosophy, economics (broadly conceived), sociology and education regarding what moral education may look like, if the authors' recommendations are taken seriously. The African philosophy of *Ubuntu/Botho* has great promise for moral education, both through its teaching and in research. Metz and Gaie analyse *Ubuntu/Botho* and offer a 'theoretical reconstruction' of an African approach to moral education research as a plausible alternative to Western approaches to morality. They make a compelling case for *Ubuntu/Botho* as worthy of attention by international moral theorists by presenting a comprehensive principle – that of social harmony and personhood. For them the goal of moral education should be to develop the personhood of students, which means facilitating their capacity to prize community. Metz also provides an important and complementary review of recent work in African ethics. Drawing on three main areas, namely how African ethics speaks to political and economic life, environmental concerns and medical practice, his review introduces the rich texts of African ethics.

Economically, Mogobe Ramose, one of Africa's foremost philosophers, presents *Ubuntu/Botho* as an antidote to the current practice of timocracy (rule by money). Analysing historical trends in gender relationships, franchise, development practice, the use of privatised military forces and the evolution of money, he shows how timocracy threatens to undermine democracy, not only in Africa but internationally. In concluding he expounds on *Ubuntu/Botho's* central tenet of valuing people over possessions and applies his thinking to everyday life in an African context. It is symbolic that this antidote to high capitalism comes from a continent where the effects of global greed and consumption are most acutely experienced in poverty, disease, inequality and corruption.

Sociologically, in my own contribution I show how social theory has had a tentative relationship with moral education, and I offer two sociological tools –the notion of 'moral ecology' and 'moral capital'– that promise theoretical and analytical value in teaching and researching moral education. It is symbolic, also, that a plea to allow social context, *including impoverished environments*, to inform research and teaching in moral education should come from Africa. Ironically, it was my graduate education in the Global North that allowed me to see so starkly this missing emphasis in moral education.

Educationally, Matemba's paper goes beyond a description of the evolution of moral education in Botswana, and offers insight into the effects of culture, religion and modern secularisation on moral education. Matemba clearly analyses the progression of moral education in Botswana (mirroring that in other locations) –from indigenous moral education that was central to public life but tended to be authoritarian, to moral education inextricably linked to Christianity, through to the challenges of introducing a secular approach in a country with strong religious foundations.

The pain of AIDS, conflict and poverty

Of course, each of the contributions described as holding promise for moral education also hints at the pain inherent in a region facing multiple challenges. The second set of three chapters and the review dealing with HIV/AIDS describe more fully what these challenges are, and how moral education might address them. Sub-Saharan Africa suffers the ignominy of having the worst AIDS pandemic in the world. Of the 33.4 million people living with HIV worldwide, 67% live in sub-Saharan Africa (UNAIDS, 2009). The moral issues that emanate from the AIDS pandemic include the effects that a group of dissident intellectuals have had on vulnerable and poorly educated people by denying its existence and causes (known as 'AIDS denialism'); the reluctant provision of anti-retroviral medication to those infected; the daily discrimination against and stigmatisation of those who are infected; and the cultural practices that exacerbate the epidemic. The contribution by Oluga, Kiragu, Mohamed and Walli provides important data, obtained from teacher educators and teacher trainees, regarding the cultural barriers to effective AIDS education in schools. In their review, as well as discussing the moral impact of AIDS denialism, DeKadt, Makusha and Richter lay out the moral dimensions of the struggle to make life-saving treatment and drug-based prevention available to the poor. They also address the moral implications of the convergence between scientific method, indigenous knowledge and cultural practice, with respect to human health and wellbeing.

The issue of conflict is a further context of pain in which moral education occurs or needs to occur. The legacies of ethnic conflict, genocide and Apartheid, are evident in many countries of the sub-region. Moral education has an important role to play, and Rwantabagu's short chapter on moral education in the aftermath of the Burundian genocide and Weldon's on refashioning the history curriculum after Apartheid in South Africa are important contributions. Weldon focuses on the transformation required of teachers who teach the moral lessons of the past through the new history curriculum in a new South Africa. In contrast, Rwantabagu provides a commentary on the community embeddedness of moral education. While he may not have addressed the many debates surrounding modern versus traditional values, and religious versus secular values, nevertheless, he does provide an insider perspective on the future of moral (and peace) education in a region that has undergone massive and pervasive human suffering and conflict.

These contributions deserve to be widely read and discussed because of their global implications, not just, but especially, where moral education is undertaken in pluralist contexts and in the presence of economic disparity –for is that not now everywhere? Together these themes of the role of moral education in economics, conflict and culture, and a moral response to AIDS constitute the pain and the promise of doing moral education in sub-Saharan Africa. But there is further anguish for moral education in Africa; it concerns the state of academic scholarship in the region.

The state of African scholarship on morality

African scholarship as a whole faces enormous challenges. These include an academic brain drain to the Global North, little interest in African publishing by international publishers, even less opportunity for African academics to publish given the pressures of academic teaching in under-resourced institutions, and limited access to current scholarship through publications, the Internet and due to the high costs of intra-continental travel. These challenges are similarly experienced in African moral education scholarship and have affected the circumstances under which this volume has been produced. Many contributions that were received were in need of deeper thought, clearer argument and more precise expression. Over the past two years, many of the chapters now in this volume have been refined beyond what is usual for an international publication. For this I am indebted to the journal editor (Monica Taylor), my research assistants (Valerie Anderson and Ingrid van der Heijden) and to the twenty referees whose names appear in *Notes on Contributors*. Even so, a few important contributions could not be completed due to competing demands, or, in the end, a lack of capacity. Thus this edited collection is an *initial* attempt to bring some of the current work in moral education in sub-Saharan Africa to wider attention and an attempt to encourage scholarship on moral education in Africa.

There remain a number of gaps in African moral education scholarship. There are as yet few empirically evaluated success stories about peace, citizenship, sex or moral education which address the deep challenges of this region. Neither are there documented and analysed examples of countries that have managed to implement progressive, contextual programmes of scale. Unlike the case in the Global North, where psychological approaches to moral education predominate, there are also no obvious contributions from scholars working in moral psychology *in an African context*. It is hoped that this volume will be a catalyst to endeavours in these and other areas of moral education with an African perspective.

The seven chapters and two reviews in this volume are written by 14 contributors from seven countries: Botswana (1), Burundi (1), Kenya (1), Malawi (1), South Africa (7), Tanzania (2) and Zimbabwe (1). While contributors are not representative of the sub-region, much less the continent, their numbers and country representation extend the group of participants from six countries who met for the first time in September 2008 at the inaugural meeting of the African Moral Education Network held in Cape Town, under the sponsorship of the *Journal of Moral Education (JME)* and the Human Sciences Research Council, South Africa. Moreover, this edition, more than doubles, in one volume, the number of contributions from Africa which the *JME* has been able to publish in the almost forty years of its existence. Until now there have been only six published papers, written by Africans or dealing with Africa (Potgieter, 1980; McCormick, 1980; Lawrence, 1982; Verhoef & Michel, 1997; Swartz, 2006; Haste & Abrahams, 2008).

For too long, moral education scholarship (as with most areas of scholarship) has been centred in the Global North. This volume offers a small corrective and provides thought-provoking and challenging ways in which contributions from the Global South impacts on wider contexts of moral education. A key measure of success in offering to *JME* readers 'another voice', a distinctive sub-Saharan voice, is *response*. My co-contributors and I invite critique, challenge, debate, engagement anything but silence – since, from the perspective of sub-Saharan Africa, that would be further cultural imperialism, and at its core an act of immorality.

References

Crais, C.C. (2002) The politics of evil: magic, state power, and the political imagination in South Africa (Cambridge, UK, Cambridge University Press).

Haste, H. & Abrahams, S. (2008) Morality, culture and the dialogic self: taking cultural pluralism seriously, *Journal of Moral Education*, 37(3), 377-394.

Krog, A. (1999) *Country of my skull* (London, Vintage).

Lawrence, M. (1982) Moral education or indoctrination in South Africa? A brief response to Potgieter, *Journal of Moral Education*, 11(3), 188-191.

McCormick, R. (1980) Political education as moral education in Tanzania, *Journal of Moral Education*, 9(3), 166-177.

Potgieter, P. C. (1980) Moral education in South Africa, *Journal of Moral Education*, 9(2), 130-133.

Republic of South Africa. Parliament (1950) *The Immorality Act* (No. 21 of 1950) (Pretoria, Government Printer).

Swartz, S. (2006) A long walk to citizenship: morality, justice and faith in the aftermath of apartheid, *Journal of Moral Education*, 35(4), 551-570.

Stanford Encyclopaedia of Philosophy (2006) *Colonialism* Available online at: http://plato.stanford.edu/entries/colonialism (accessed 22 May 2010).

Truth and Reconciliation Commission (1999) Truth and Reconciliation Commission of South Africa report. Volume one (London, Macmillan).

UNAIDS (2009) Fact sheet. Available online at: http://data.unaids.org/pub/FactSheet/2009/20091124_FS_SSA_en.pdf(accessed 21 May 2010).

Verhoef, H. & Michel, C. (1997) Studying morality within the African context: a model of moral analysis and construction, *Journal of Moral Education*, 26(4), 389-407.

The African ethic of *Ubuntu/Botho*: implications for research on morality

Thaddeus Metz[a] and Joseph B.R. Gaie[b]

[a]*University of Johannesburg, South Africa;* [b]*University of Botswana, Botswana*

In this article we provide a theoretical reconstruction of sub-Saharan ethics that we argue is a strong competitor to typical Western approaches to morality. According to our African moral theory, actions are right roughly insofar as they are a matter of living harmoniously with others or honouring communal relationships. After spelling out this ethic, we apply it to several issues in both normative and empirical research into morality. With regard to normative research, we compare and contrast this African moral theory with utilitarianism and Kantianism in the context of several practical issues. With regard to empirical research, we compare and contrast our sub-Saharan ethic with several of Lawrence Kohlberg's views on the nature of morality. Our aim is to highlight respects in which the African approach provides a unitary foundation for a variety of normative and empirical conclusions that are serious alternatives to dominant Western views.

Introduction

How should children be morally educated? How should a society respond to moral infraction? Is there a universal logic to moral development? Is there a plausible alternative to the justice and care models of moral reasoning and action? In this article, we answer these and other important questions about morality by appealing to sub-Saharan values. Partly, our aim is to acquaint an international audience with African ideas, but we also maintain that, suitably refined, they provide perspectives that genuinely compete with those characteristic of the Western tradition.

We begin by sketching the basic elements of a major strain of sub-Saharan moral thought, which we call 'Afro-communitarianism'. Then we apply this conception of morality to some central issues in normative research, highlighting respects in which its implications differ from those of influential Western perspectives, especially Kantian and utilitarian moral theories. Next, we apply our Afro-communitarian theory to key issues in empirical research, again highlighting respects in which its implications differ from those of important Western social science, using the work of Lawrence Kohlberg as a foil. Our purpose is not merely to compare, but also to advocate; we aim to show that sub-Saharan values are unjustly neglected in global debates among moral theorists.

Whenever writing on Africa, one is expected to note the diversity of the continent, with more than 50 countries and at least several hundred ethnic groups and languages. Because of the variety of sources available, we have had to obtain focus in this article, with two factors influencing our choice of materials. First, there is our basic aim, which is to indicate how an indigenous African perspective might reasonably motivate a scholar anywhere in the world to change her understanding of how to conduct normative or empirical research on morality. There are ideas in traditional sub-Saharan Africa that overlap with ones common in contemporary Western moral thought (e.g. Prinsloo, 1998, p. 48) but we have downplayed these in order to highlight ways in which the international field of moral education might have something to learn from underrepresented ideas from below the Sahara desert. Furthermore, there are ideas in sub-Saharan Africa that are so far removed from non-African contexts as to be 'beyond the pale' for many scholars interested in moral research, a good example being widespread beliefs among Africans about the existence of ancestors in a spiritual realm who interact with us. These ideas, too, we sidestep, despite the fact that many Africans deem them essential to their worldview.

A second factor affecting our focus in this article is our backgrounds as moral philosophers living in southern Africa. Much of our discussion is a matter of bringing philosophical insights to bear on normative and empirical issues and, as we are most familiar with southern African worldviews and languages, we concentrate on them. We note, however, that most scholars of the sub-Saharan region maintain that, while there is substantial diversity among its traditional cultures, there are also threads that many share. So, while we discuss *an* (not *the*) African theory of morality, we are confident that many, if not most, other peoples below the Sahara would find it familiar and attractive.

Afro-Communitarianism[1]

A good starting point for understanding sub-Saharan morality, or the major strand of it that we explore, is the phrase, 'A person is a person through other persons' or 'I am because we are'. In southern African languages, this would be, '*Motho ke motho ka batho babang*' in Sotho-Tswana and '*Umuntu ngumuntu ngabantu*' in the Nguni languages of Zulu, Xhosa or Ndebele. Most people in Botswana, South Africa and Zimbabwe speak either one of these languages or a language related to them. However, the phrase is not restricted to these languages and many sub-Saharan societies have versions of it in their respective languages. The Kenyan John Mbiti (1969), in his classic survey of African worldviews, takes the phrase to be a 'cardinal point in the African view of man' (pp. 108–109) and a large majority of scholars agree with him on this score.

To most international readers, 'A person is a person through other persons' will bring to mind nothing prescriptive and, instead, will indicate merely some descriptive claims about the dependence of a human being, particularly a child, on other human beings for her survival or for the course her life takes. The phrase does connote empirical facts of this sort, as well as, for many Africans, metaphysical ideas about the interdependence of all beings in the universe. However, the phrase also carries an important normative connotation. Personhood, identity and humanness in characteristic sub-Saharan language and thought are value-laden concepts. That is, one can be more or less of a person, self or human being, where the more one is, the better (Wiredu, 1992a; Menkiti, 2004). One's ultimate goal should be to become a *full* person, a *real* self or a *genuine* human being.

So construed, sub-Saharan morality is a 'self-realisation' or 'perfectionist' ethic, akin to Aristotelianism. However, there are two facets that arguably make an African approach distinctive. First, sub-Saharan morality is *essentially* relational in a way that other Western approaches usually are not. That is, in a typical African ethic, the *only* way to develop one's humanness is to relate to others in a positive way. One becomes a person solely 'through other persons', which means that one cannot realise one's true self in opposition to others or even in isolation from them. As Augustine Shutte (2001), one of the first professional philosophers to seriously engage with *Ubuntu/Botho*, says, 'Our deepest moral obligation is to become more fully human. And this means entering more and more deeply into community with others. So although the goal is personal fulfilment, selfishness is excluded' (p. 30). Consequently, prudence is ruled out as a source of virtue, along with any purely self-regarding activity, such as rationally controlling one's appetites or contemplating basic features of the universe for its own sake, characteristically Greek ideals (see Plato's *Republic* [trans. Grube, 1974] or Aristotle's *Nicomachean ethics* [trans. Irwin, 2000]). If one harms others, e.g. by being exploitive, deceptive or unfaithful, or even if one is merely indifferent to others and fails to share oneself with them, then one is said to be lacking '*Botho*' (Sotho-Tswana) or '*Ubuntu*' (Nguni), literally lacking in personhood or humanness.[2] In the way that 'an unjust law is no law at all' (as per Augustine's *On free choice of the will* [trans. Williams, 1993]) or just as we might say that a jalopy is 'not a *real* car' (Gaie, 2007, p. 33), so Africans would say of an individual who does not relate positively to others that 'he is not a person'. Indeed, those without much *Ubuntu/Botho* are often described as animals (Pearce, 1990, p. 147; Bhengu, 1996, p. 27; Letseka, 2000, p. 186).

A second respect in which African morality characteristically differs from an Aristotelian or other Western moral philosophy concerns the way it defines a positive relationship with others, namely, in strictly *communal* terms. One is not to positively relate to others fundamentally by giving them what they deserve, respecting individual rights grounded on consent, participating in a political sphere or maximising the general welfare, common themes in Western moral philosophy. Instead, the proper way to relate to others, for one large part of sub-Saharan thinking, is to seek out community or to live in harmony with them (for representative statements, see Biko, 1971/2004, p. 46; Silberbauer, 1991, p. 20; Verhoef & Michel, 1997, p. 397; Kasenene, 1998, p. 21; Tutu, 1999, p. 35; Mkhize, 2008, pp. 38–41).

To seek out community (harmony) with others is not merely the notion of doing whatever a majority of people in society want or of adhering to the norms of one's group, which are influential forms of relativism and communitarianism in the West (e.g. Harman, 1975; Walzer, 1983). Instead, from our African viewpoint, developing or respecting community (harmony) is an objectively desirable kind of interaction that should instead guide what majorities want or which norms become dominant.

As one of us has argued elsewhere (Metz, 2007), there are two recurrent themes in typical African discussion of the nature of community or harmony. First, there is the idea that one has a moral obligation to be concerned for the good of others, in terms of both one's sympathetic emotional reactions toward other people and one's helpful behaviour toward them. In short, one has a duty to exhibit solidarity with others. Second, there is the idea that one has a moral obligation to think of oneself as bound up with others, that is, to define oneself as a member of a common group and to participate in its practices. One also has a duty to identify with others. Community or harmony is the *combination* of both solidarity and identity, so construed. One finds implicit references to both elements in the following illustrative statements about community (harmony): 'Every member is expected to consider him/herself an integral part of the whole and to play an appropriate role towards achieving the good of all' (Gbadegesin, 1991, p. 65); 'Harmony is achieved through close and sympathetic social relations within the group' (Mokgoro, 1998, p. 3); 'The fundamental meaning of community is the sharing of an overall way of life, inspired by the notion of the common good' (Gyekye, 2004, p. 16); '[T]he purpose of our life is community-service and community-belongingness' (Iroegbu, 2005, p. 442).

The combination of exhibiting solidarity with others and of identifying with them is more or less what is meant by a broad sense of 'friendliness' or 'love', essential to an ideal sort of family. So, another way to understand African morality is in terms of esteeming familial relationships. As Shutte (2001) notes, 'The extended family is probably the most common, and also the most fundamental, expression of the African idea of community. ...The importance of this idea for ethics is that the family is something that is valued for its own sake' (p. 29). Familial relationships of the right sort have good consequences for individuals, but the fascinating idea salient in sub-Saharan morality is the notion that they are to be morally valued in themselves, apart from their results. One is obligated to prize one's existing familial relationships and also to promote them wherever one reasonably can, so that all human beings are seen as potential members of an ideal family, that is, as individuals to be loved.

Such a conception of ethics is reminiscent of a certain strain of Christian morality and a fair 'armchair anthropology' would suggest that Christianity spread so easily in sub-Saharan Africa because of its fit with a traditional moral outlook. Note, however, that most friends of a sub-Saharan ethic do not conceive of it strictly impartially, in the way that a Christian might of *agape*. Instead, one's actual friendly relationships have a moral priority over relationships one could have in the future and over those of which one neither is nor would be a part. 'Family first' and 'charity begins at home' are recurrent maxims of African moral thinking, where, at a fundamental level, the agent's own, existing communal relationships are given precedence over others (Appiah, 1998).

We reiterate that this sketch of an Afro-communitarian moral perspective should not be taken to represent anthropologically the beliefs of Africans about the right way to live. It is, rather, a theoretical reconstruction of themes that are recurrent among many peoples below the Sahara desert and particularly in southern Africa. However, this Afro-communitarian principle, which prescribes prizing friendly relationships, should be attractive to a much wider audience—for it is plausible, even if underexplored, to think of actions such as theft, deception, cruelty and the like as being wrong just to the extent that they are *unfriendly*.

Implications of *Ubuntu/Botho* for normative research

To make the *Ubuntu/Botho* viewpoint more concrete, and to indicate how it could affect research into morality, in this section we bring out some of *Ubuntu/Botho*'s unique implications for prescribing actions and policies as morally right (and then, in the following section, we discuss what *Ubuntu/Botho* entails for describing people's moral behaviour). Specifically, we consider some of the normative implications of *Ubuntu/Botho* for the distribution of property, criminal justice, medical practice, family life and moral education. We have selected these topics because they cover a wide array of different situations, because they facilitate clear contrasts between *Ubuntu/Botho* and the Western ethical principles of utility and of respect and because other topics are covered elsewhere in this issue.[3]

The distribution of property

Western practice and philosophy grounds the distribution of property largely on an individualist model. Generally, a person is deemed rightful owner of land or other wealth if he acquired it without harming others, for example by having created it himself from un-owned materials or by having received it from another rightful owner who made a voluntary decision to bestow it upon him, say, in exchange for labour or as part of an inheritance. When taxation of property is permitted, it is usually done in order to meet the basic needs of the poor or to enable them to obtain the education or other qualifications needed to compete for work. Kantians often think that such a model of property distribution respects people's autonomy, while utilitarians tend to think that this model produces wealth and hence satisfies interests better than other models.

In contrast to this distributive approach based largely on individual choices made in labour and consumer markets, *Ubuntu/Botho* prescribes distributing property in a way that expresses esteem for communal relationships. One implication of such a relational focus is much less of a tolerance for economic inequality than what is typical in the West, for a sense of togetherness is difficult to foster when some have much greater wealth than others (Magesa, 1997, pp. 277–278). A second implication of *Ubuntu/Botho*'s focus on harmony is that membership in the community is, by and large, sufficient to be entrusted with an adequate portion of its land or other major kinds of wealth (traditionally cattle), supposing one continues to make good use of it and does not let it go to waste (Gyekye, 1997, pp. 146–152, 160–161; Magesa, 1997, pp. 279–282). A third implication is that every moral agent has particularly weighty duties to aid his family, which includes many extended members, such as in-laws, uncles and cousins (Gyekye, 1997, pp. 61–75; Masolo, 2004, p. 494). Indeed, in traditional Setswana society, for example, it would be considered theft if one slaughtered an animal and kept the meat for oneself or gave it only to one's nuclear family. Note that it does not obviously follow from *Ubuntu/Botho* that markets are unjust, particularly if they would be most efficient at creating wealth for the community. However, it is clear that if markets are justified, they are to be constrained to a much greater degree than they usually are in the West.[4]

Criminal justice

In Western societies, there are two dominant rationales for state punishment of adult offenders: retribution and deterrence. The retributive rationale, often associated with a Kantian morality, is the view that punishment is justified simply as a fitting response to the nature of the crime that was committed, that is, merely because the offender deserves it for what he has done. The deterrence rationale, naturally at home in a utilitarian ethic, is the view that punishment is justified as a way to instil fear in the offender and others so that they will avoid committing other crimes in the future. Although one will find retributive and deterrence elements in the behaviour of traditional African societies, one finds an additional salient approach taken in them, and neither retribution nor deterrence is particularly what *Ubuntu/Botho* would prescribe.

Specifically, reconciliation, that is, the reparation of broken relationships, as the aim of criminal justice is a major theme among friends of *Ubuntu/Botho* (Magesa, 1997, pp. 234–240, 267–276; Tutu, 1999; Bell, 2002, 85–107; Louw, 2006; Krog, 2008). Sometimes punishment is eschewed altogether in favour of apology and compensation, while at other times, when punishment is imposed, it is done with an eye to resolving conflict between the offender and his victims or between his family and the families of those whom he has wronged. Rather than intentionally create a climate of fear (utilitarian deterrence) or impose harm merely for its own sake (Kantian retribution), *Ubuntu/Botho* in the first instance recommends seeking restorative justice, using punishment only when necessary to foster the good of harmonious relationships.

Medical practice

For one example in a healthcare context, consider the question of whether an individual patient has the right to expect that medical professionals will keep private information about her diagnosis and treatment. It is standard in the West to think that a patient has the right to confidentiality with regard to her healthcare, either because it would be degrading to reveal intimate details without her consent (Kantianism) or because such revelation would damage trust between her and healthcare workers and hence impair her health (utilitarianism).

In contrast, the privacy of an individual patient probably will not be as weighty in an Afro-communitarian ethic. Because individuals are understood to have weighty duties to aid others, particularly family members, it is not merely up to the individual what she does with her body and mind. Since other members of the community have a stake in the individual's health, many Africans would think that they ought to be aware of her illness and play a role in discussing how she ought to treat it (Kasenene, 2000, pp. 349–353, 356; Murove, 2005, pp. 170–171; Dube, 2009, pp. 192–199). It does not obviously follow that coercive or deceptive paternalism is justified by *Ubuntu/Botho*; but it does seem to follow from this ethic that an individual's illness is a collective affair to some degree, that is, that considerations of confidentiality have less moral significance than in the typical Western approach.

Family life

It is common in the West to think that once one has married another person, one has a moral obligation not to break one's vows. In addition, it is typical there to believe that, once one has had children, one has a moral obligation to ensure that they are cared for, even if one does not do the rearing oneself. These obligations are also entailed by an African ethic, but it goes beyond them in important ways.

In particular, an Afro-communitarian morality will likely prescribe both getting married and having children in the first place (Wiredu, 1992b, p. 205; Magesa, 1997, pp. 63, 89, 120–121, 167; Bujo, 2001, pp. 6–7, 34–54). While in the West marriage is often seen as an optional matter for an individual, *Ubuntu/Botho* as articulated here entails that one has a basic duty to wed, and many African societies believe in such a duty. After all, seeking out community with others would seem to mean creating the most intimate forms of interaction one can with someone, viz., romantic love, or at least a personal relationship formed in the course of living with others. Furthermore, many African societies believe that one has a basic duty to create children. Again, if communal relationships are to be prized, then one has some moral obligation to make ones in which there is a robust sharing of life and caring for it. These are stark contrasts with dominant Western moral perspectives, for remaining single and childless would appear neither to disrespect anyone's autonomy (Kantianism) nor to fail to maximise the average amount of well-being (utilitarianism).

Moral education

What is it that a moral educator ought to teach and how ought she to teach it? The default position among contemporary Western pedagogical theorists is that the morally correct approach to ethical teaching and learning involves appealing to the student's rationality and raising a cosmopolitan awareness of different value systems. When dealing with morality in the classroom, Western values entail doing so in a way that engages the student's capacity for critical deliberation and does not restrict the relevant perspectives to those of the student's own culture, leaving it up to the student which values she will adopt. Such an approach is respectful of the student's autonomy (Kantianism) and promises to maximise the happiness of the student and those with whom she interacts (utilitarianism).

Moral education in traditional African communities has typically been on the opposite pole. Moral education among indigenous sub-Saharan societies has usually been parochial, focused exclusively on imparting the norms of the student's culture, and moral educators have often used fear and indoctrination to instil values, dissuading students from questioning the (often gendered) roles being handed down (Pearce, 1990; Adeyemi & Adeyinka, 2003; Ikuenobe, 2006, pp. 135–255; also Matemba, this issue, pp. 329–343). The standard justification for these approaches is that they are effective at obtaining the desired behaviour, viz., preserving culture (in a non-literate society) and exhibiting virtue.

We maintain that *Ubuntu/Botho*, as theoretically construed above, prescribes an approach that differs from the characteristically Western and the traditionally African. *Ubuntu/Botho* in the first instance entails that the goal of moral education should be to develop the personhood of students, which means facilitating their capacity to prize community. Since that, in turn, means giving some moral weight to *existing* communal relationships, it would indeed be incumbent on a moral educator not only to inform students of their duty not to radically upset norms central to the community's self-conception, but also to focus on transmitting these values.

However, it does not follow that moral education is simply a matter of ensuring students mimic the past, for three reasons. First, being concerned for the good of students entails not utterly restricting their knowledge to that of a fairly circumscribed culture, particularly in a globalised world in which even rural communities have to engage with a wide array of foreign people, policies and institutions. It is implausible to think a given culture at a particular moment is optimal, or even adequate, for the welfare of all the people who participate in it. So, the injunction to exhibit solidarity with others gives a moral educator reason not to quash student doubt about the propriety of an existing way of life. Second, in order to genuinely *share* a way of life, a moral educator ought not to rely on threats and rote regurgitation. Truly sharing a way of life means voluntarily participating in it, for part of what is valuable about a loving or friendly relationship is the fact that people come together, and stay together, of their own accord. Third, since becoming a person includes caring about the quality of others' lives, a moral educator needs to help develop students' capacity for sympathy and encourage them to engage in mutual aid with themselves, their extended families and the broader society.

Implications of *Ubuntu/Botho* for empirical research

In the previous section, we noted several respects in which, upon taking *Ubuntu/Botho* seriously as a normative theory, one's views of what moral agents may or may not do change substantially. Here, we shift from prescriptive issues to descriptive ones, indicating ways in which social scientific understanding of moral behaviour would differ, in light of an Afro-communitarian interpretation of right action. In order to bring out the implications of *Ubuntu/Botho*, which are often attractive, we contrast them with

Kohlberg's system. Although we are aware that much of Kohlberg's framework has been seriously questioned,[5] it plays such a dominant role in systematic empirical thinking about morality that it is useful to orient debate. In the following, we address four topics central to Kohlberg's account of morality, namely, the nature of moral development, of moral reasoning and action, of moral motivation and of moral knowledge. With regard to Kohlberg's views on these topics, we rely heavily on his last major statement of them (1986).

Moral development

The question, here, is how to characterise the process of moral maturation and, in particular, whether there is any kind of moral growth that occurs universally, viz., in all human societies. Famously, according to Kohlberg, human beings, as they mature from children to adults under normal circumstances, tend to develop their thinking about interpersonal moral considerations in a series of invariant stages, with later stages being improvements over earlier ones. Interpersonal morality has to do with conflicts of interest between two or more persons and so excludes the morality of duties to oneself or to non-persons. Kohlberg's hypothesis with regard to such considerations is that human cognition can be expected to progress in six stages, and while Kohlberg did not empirically confirm the existence of a sixth stage (Kohlberg, 1984, p. 270), he clearly thinks of it as the highest form of moral awareness about justice that human beings could be expected to obtain and it has been very influential in the field. We therefore use it as a foil.

At Stage Six, people think about conflicts of interest in terms of the equal consideration of all persons. More specifically, resolving conflicts among people in the most defensible manner requires teasing out the implications of a procedural principle that even-handedly represents everyone as having a say about, or a stake in, the outcome. John Rawls's (1971) hypothetical social contract theory is well-known for being a philosophical illustration of Stage Six moral reasoning for Kohlberg.

Now, *Ubuntu/Botho* fails to reach Stage Six, and by a long shot, as we shall demonstrate. In terms of laypeople's understanding of morality in sub-Saharan Africa, there is evidence that they either have failed, or clearly would fail, to approach interpersonal conflict in the purely impartial or universalising manner that Kohlberg thinks is ideal (Edwards, 1975; Miller, 1992, pp. 20–41). Furthermore, beyond the lay understanding of *Ubuntu/Botho,* not even the philosophical reconstruction articulated here would reach Stage Six. *Ubuntu/Botho* does accord all human beings a moral status and considers everyone in principle to be potential members of an ideal family based on loving or friendly relationships. Call this *Ubuntu/Botho*'s 'impartial' element. Focusing for the moment on this impartial element alone, note that it would not be enough to achieve Stage Six, since it does not include a procedure by which conflicts of interest are to be resolved by the real or imagined participation of everyone.

More problematically, however, *Ubuntu/Botho* is not purely impartial and this is so in two glaring respects. First, as indicated above, an African ethic accords, at a fundamental level, a greater moral weight to persons related in some way to the agent. In traditional African morality, kinship is the key relation, whereas in our philosophical construction, those communal relationships of which the agent is actually a part are deemed to have a higher moral importance than other relationships. Hence, *Ubuntu/Botho* implies that it would be inappropriate *invariably* to tackle interpersonal moral dilemmas in a *purely* impartial way. Instead, the fact that certain people are related to the agent in a communal way can provide some reason to resolve conflicts of interest in one way rather than another.

For example, in the famous Heinz case, Kohlberg clearly deems it merely Stage Three moral reflection for Heinz to appeal to the fact that *he loves* his wife as a moral reason to steal a drug that is necessary and sufficient for her to stay alive (Kohlberg, 1986, pp. 493, 501, 528). Stage Six reasoning would explicitly exclude the fact of an affectionate partial relationship as a reason to steal the drug and would instead appeal, for example, to the fact that the druggist could not reasonably reject, on grounds of an interest in taking advantage of superior bargaining power, a claim on behalf of another person to stay alive. *Ubuntu/Botho* might well include such impartial reasoning (e.g. Ramose, 1999, pp. 181–190), but it implies that it does not exhaust the relevant moral considerations. In fact, relying solely on such reasoning might be unjust, for *Ubuntu/Botho*, in that it fails to recognise the greater importance of one's wife.

A second respect in which *Ubuntu/Botho* is not purely impartial is that it resolves conflicts of interest in part by appealing to existing configurations of relationships. Whereas in Kohlberg's framework, a moral decision ideally is one that judges any existing relationship entirely in light of a procedure that gives everyone's interests equal representation, in an African ethic the bare fact of tradition has *some* moral weight that needs to be balanced against other, more welfare-oriented concerns. Where a people's identity is constituted by certain practices, it is a morally relevant consideration that their sense of themselves as a group would be upset by changing these practices. So, in the context of the Heinz dilemma, if one approach were inconsistent with a people's sense of 'who we are', that would be some reason to reject it, by *Ubuntu/Botho*.

What does the difference between Kohlberg's Stage Six and our conception of *Ubuntu/Botho* entail for moral development? One might suggest a pluralist account of moral maturation, according to which it differs depending on the nature of the society one is in. For example, some suggest that Kohlberg's model is apt for a modern, urban society, whereas an ethic that prizes communal relationship is appropriate for a small-scale society in which there are few strangers (Edwards, 1975; Verhoef & Michel, 1997).

There is, however, another, bolder conclusion one could reasonably draw, namely, that there is a monistic, universal logic to moral maturation, where Kohlberg's conception of Stage Six and *Ubuntu/Botho* are competing accounts of its ultimate end. Some reason for taking *Ubuntu/Botho* seriously as the telos of moral development is the massive upswing of interest among contemporary moral philosophers in the limitations of impartiality. In Kohlberg's heyday, analytic ethicists were drawn to conceiving the 'moral point of view' in strictly impartial terms (e.g., Frankena, 1963; Baier, 1965) and he is well known for having drawn on their discussion to ground his conception of morality. These days, however, many philosophers acknowledge a need to incorporate norms of intimacy and tradition into fundamental moral thinking about how to resolve conflicts of interest (see, for just a few examples, Sandel, 1984; Scheffler, 2001; Jeske, 2008; Feltham & Cottingham, 2010).

Moral reasoning and action

Those in the field of moral education in recent years have tended to divide up conceptions of permissible other-regarding reflection and behaviour in terms of justice and care orientations. A justice approach is one that conceives of a moral agent's obligations to others fundamentally in terms of individual rights, whereas, in a care model, they are constituted by relationships that include some kind of recipro-cal interaction, typically in which one cares for others and they respond in some positive way to one because of one's caring. Kohlberg is typically thought to represent a justice perspective, thinking of moral action in terms of respect for the equal rights of individuals. An Afro-communitarian conception of moral reasoning and action, as we now demonstrate, can be reduced to neither one of these perspectives. It not only incorporates elements from both in an elegant way (a point others sometimes make e.g. Ikuenobe, 2006, p. 116), but also, we contend, includes elements that transcend both and that should be given serious consideration.

With regard to the justice orientation, *Ubuntu/Botho* is similar in that it does include an impartial element, part of which is a matter of individual rights. Traditional African societies have often thought of human life as having a dignity that implies recognition of certain universal human rights. For instance, despite the moral prominence given to their own community, indigenous sub-Saharan societies are well-known for having welcomed a stranger to their villages, giving him food and shelter for at least a short period. They hardly considered a foreigner outside the bounds of moral consideration and, instead, tended to view all humans as potential parts of an ideal family.

However, *Ubuntu/Botho* is far from exhausted by impartial, rights-based consider-ations. This is so in at least three respects. First, we have already noted the intimacy element of Afro-communitarianism. Conflicts of interest should not always be resolved purely by appeal to human rights, but also, in part, by considerations of whether a given person is communally related to the agent, in a way that need not be grounded in universal norms of promise-making. Second, we have also noted that *Ubuntu/Botho* accords some weight to historical factors that are not reducible to individual rights. An existing way of life that is salient in a group's self-conception has some moral significance, for Afro-communitarianism. Third, an African conception of morality will likely include duties to aid others without correlative rights (see, especially, Gyekye, 1997, pp. 61–75). To see this, consider ideal family norms. Suppose that your family has divided up a pot of stew either equally or in accordance with some agreement, but that your brother turns out to be dissatisfied with his share.

Imagine that he does not downright need another bowlful, but would greatly appreciate one. And suppose that the last amount is in your possession by the original division and that you do not particularly want it. On a pure individual rights model, you would be permitted to eat the remaining stew, or even to throw it away, but *Ubuntu/Botho* would probably entail that you would instead have an obligation to give it to your brother. Similar remarks apply to the way people not in one's (nuclear) family ought to interact.

With regard to a care model, *Ubuntu/Botho* is similar in that it morally values relationships above all and, in particular, existing ones that include emotional and practical concern for others' well-being. So far it sounds indistinguishable from the classic ethic of care of Nel Noddings (1984) and some theorists have suggested that African morality is not qualitatively different from such an ethic (e.g. Harding, 1987/ 1998). However, this ethic of care is strictly partial in a way that, as we have seen, *Ubuntu/Botho* is not. In the standard care ethic, one has a duty to aid others only if they can respond positively to the one aiding, that is, only if they can help to create a reciprocal relationship, something that distant, starving people cannot (Noddings, 1984, pp. 86, 89). An Afro-communitarian model does not restrict moral obligation in this way; again, all human beings are deemed part of a family who provide some reason to be responded to out of love.

Even if the ethic of care were interpreted more broadly, so as not to require mutuality between a care-giver and one who in some way appreciatively accepts this care (cf. Noddings, 1992, pp. 110–112; Donovan & Adams, 2007), there would still be a major difference between it and *Ubuntu/Botho*. According to Afro-communitarianism, the relevant relationship to prize is not merely one of caring for others' quality of life but, in addition, sharing a way of life. A fundamental moral value for *Ubuntu/Botho* is identification with others, that is, enjoying a sense of togetherness and coordinating behaviour to realise common goals. Care does not exhaust either the nature or value of a friendly or communal relationship.

If the reader finds *Ubuntu/Botho prima facie* attractive, then the typical dichotomy between justice and care needs to be viewed as much too restrictive. Not all plausible conceptions of moral reflection and behaviour can be reduced to either one of these or even to a combination of them.

Moral motivation

On any attractive view of what it is that moves an agent to perform right actions, or at least those that confer virtue on him, both self-regarding and other-regarding elements will play a role. This is true of Kohlberg's account of moral motivation, which is less well known than other features of his system. According to him, there can be times when an agent performs a moral action for the self-regarding reason of wanting the self-respect associated with doing the right thing (Kohlberg, 1986, pp. 498–499). However, right behaviour, properly construed, is a matter of acting consequent to an awareness of the results of an impartial procedure for adjudicating competing claims; a moral action, most often and fundamentally, is the product of a conscious apprehension of an other-regarding consideration. That is, moral motivation on Kohlberg's model is characteristically a Kantian matter of doing right by the other because it is right.

Ubuntu/Botho cashes out the self- and other-regarding elements of moral motivation differently. With regard to the self, one's most basic obligation is to develop one's humanness. This is an evaluative, rather than normative, ideal. That is, instead of wanting to perform an action merely for the sake of duty, as per Kohlberg, an African ethic would construe one's basic motivation with regard to the self in terms of wanting to be a real human being or to obtain complete personhood.

With regard to others, as we have seen, *Ubuntu/Botho* does not deem the moral worth of an action inherently to be a product of cognition about strictly impartial norms. Becoming a full person or real self is to prize communal relationships, particularly existing ones of which the agent is a part. Moreover, this ethic would likely deem cognition not to be exhaustive of, or perhaps even sufficient for, the factors that move one to perform a right or virtuous action. Recall that communal relationships themselves include an emotional engagement with others' well-being, often cashed out in terms of sympathy. Acting out of sympathy is part of what is called for when acting rightly or virtuously, for the Afro-communitarian moral theory we have spelled out. Such a view accords the emotions a constitutive role in moral motivation that is, notoriously, lacking in Kohlberg's model, where the emotions are merely tools for facilitating cognitive awareness of the impartial 'moral point of view', which is what causes properly moral action (Kohlberg, 1986, p. 499).

Moral knowledge

What is it that one knows when one understands morality and how does one come to grasp it? Kohlberg's answer is well known: to understand morality, in its highest sense, is to understand a certain procedural principle, perhaps as applied to a given context, and the way one comes to be aware of this principle and its practical implications is by conscious, rational deliberation. It follows from Kohlberg's model that people in at least their 30s and 40s could exhibit a deep moral understanding, viz., some post-conventional morality, even if none of Kohlberg's longitudinal participants ever reached Stage Six and few unambiguously achieved Stage Five (Kohlberg, 1984, Ch. 6).

To begin to draw a contrast with *Ubuntu/Botho*, consider that friends of this ethic hold that it is only elders who attain full personhood, implying that only they are capable of moral wisdom. One of the most influential African moral philosophers, the Nigerian Ifeanyi Menkiti (2004), makes these comments:

> Hence the Igbo African proverb: 'What an old man sees sitting down, a young man cannot see standing up.'…[A]lthough we would not have a great deal of difficulty talking about an 18-year-old mathematical giant, we would have a great deal of difficulty talking about an 18-year-old moral giant. (p. 325)

Which sort of moral epistemology would underwrite this recurrent judgement among Africans? What would moral knowledge have to be like in order for a robust degree of it to be possible only upon quite a long 'lived experience' (Setiloane, 1976, p. 40; Menkiti, 2004, pp. 325, 326)?

While, for Kohlberg, lived experience is indeed necessary for moral wisdom, this is so principally insofar as it is a matter of improving one's *reasoning*, for example, considering others' viewpoints in order to find a principled way to resolve moral problems (Kohlberg, 1976), something that one could achieve prior to one's 50s or 60s.[6] For *Ubuntu/Botho*, however, lived experience is necessary for moral wisdom for different reasons. An Afro-communitarian morality is naturally understood to involve two types of experience-dependent moral knowledge that go beyond the baldly abstract propositional model that Kohlberg advocates.

First, to have *Ubuntu/Botho* means prizing communal relationships, but this statement belies an enormous complexity that cannot be expressly captured in a simple principle. We have noted a variety of elements that constitute the relevant sort of communal relationship, including being sympathetic to others, acting in ways that are expected to benefit them, thinking of oneself as a member of a group, behaving in ways that do not upset traditional practices and so on, where these often must be traded off against one another. In addition, we have encountered, implicitly or explicitly, distinctions between local and non-local relationships, relationships of which the agent is a part and of which she is not, actual and future relationships, and prizing harmonious relationships in the context of the actions one takes and in the context of their expected consequences. Appreciating the relevance of all these factors and learning how to balance them in a given situation plausibly requires *judgement* (and not merely reason), which, in turn, requires substantial engagement with a variety of real-life moral issues and rich narratives, available only to those of a certain age.

In addition to judgement, becoming a real person plausibly requires the adoption of certain attitudes, emotions and, more generally, ways of behaving that do not come easily. That is, in addition to knowing *that*, *Ubuntu/Botho* involves knowing *how*, certain social skills that typically take a long time to acquire. It can take a lot of work to learn how, for example, to overcome resentment toward others, to cultivate empathetic awareness of what it is like to be others, to be patient when listening to others, to be emotionally supportive of others, to be assertive in respectful ways, to forgo benefits to oneself when they would cost others and to be painfully honest with oneself about one's own motivations. If marriages are not easy, it is sometimes all the more difficult to exhibit these traits, essential to communal/harmonious/friendly relationships, in the context of people one does not know nearly as well. Hence, it would be reasonable to expect to find them truly exhibited only in an elder.

Conclusion

In this article, we have provided a theoretical reconstruction of several ideas associated with talk of '*Ubuntu/Botho*', terms that designate an indigenous sub-Saharan approach to morality. Specifically, we first articulated the Afro-communitarian principle that an action is right insofar as it prizes harmonious relationships, where harmony is a matter of both exhibiting solidarity with others and identifying with them. Then, we applied this principle to several normative issues in order to illustrate not only how it differs from salient Western theories of right action, but also how its prescriptions are often attractive. Key examples were that *Ubuntu/Botho* prescribes seeking restorative justice consequent to a wrong having been done, in contrast to deterrence and retributive models of criminal justice, and that it instructs a moral educator to develop her students' virtue in non-dogmatic ways, in contrast to a focus on their happiness or autonomy. Then, we considered what the Afro-communitarian conception of morality entails for empirical research into people's moral behaviour, contrasting its implications with those of Kohlberg's influential framework. Highlights here included the suggestion that the final stage of moral development might not be purely impartial but rather might include giving consideration to issues of intimacy and tradition, as well as the idea that there are facets of moral action that cannot be reduced to considerations of justice and care. We recognise that many of these plausible alternatives to characteristic Western approaches to morality can already be found in the international literature. However, we submit that *Ubuntu/Botho*, as analysed in this article, is worthy of attention from international moral theorists for going beyond piecemeal criticisms and instead presenting a unified foundation for them in the form of a single, comprehensive principle.

Acknowledgements

The authors are grateful for written comments on an earlier draft received from Sharlene Swartz, Monica Taylor and two anonymous referees for the *Journal of Moral Education*, one of whom provided unusually detailed and thoughtful reflections. We have also benefited from feedback received at the inaugural conference of the African Moral Education Network (AMEN), sponsored by the *Journal of Moral Education* and the Human Sciences Research Council of South Africa, 9–11 September 2008.

Notes

1. The next two paragraphs borrow from Metz (2010, p. 83).
2. In the remainder of this article, we speak of '*Ubuntu/Botho*', conjoining two terms to connote a single concept.
3. For instance, political power, workplace organisation and environmental ethics are discussed in the review article 'Recent work in African ethics' in this Special Issue (see Metz, pp. 381–391).
4. On which see Mogobe Ramose's contribution in this Special Issue, pp. 291–303.
5. For an overview of critical work on Kohlberg, see the Special Issue of the *Journal of Moral Education* edited by Don Collins Reed (2008).
6. After all, Kohlberg suspected that some graduate students in philosophy had exemplified Stage Six reasoning (1984, pp. 272–273).

References

Adeyemi, M. & Adeyinka, A. (2003) The principles and content of African traditional education, *Educational Philosophy and Theory*, 35(4), 425–440.

Appiah, A. (1998) Ethical systems, African, in: E. Craig (Ed.) *Routledge encyclopaedia of philosophy* (London, Routledge).

Baier, K. (1965) The moral point of view: a rational basis of ethics (New York, Random House).

Bell, R. (2002) *Understanding African philosophy* (New York, Routledge).

Bhengu, M. J. (1996) *Ubuntu: the essence of democracy* (Cape Town, South Africa, Novalis Press).

Biko, S. (1971/2004) *I write what I like* (Johannesburg, Picador Africa).

Bujo, B. (2001) *Foundations of an African ethic: beyond the universal claims of Western morality* (B. McNeil, Trans.) (New York, Crossroad).

Donovan, J. & Adams, C. (Eds) (2007) *The feminist care tradition in animal ethics: a reader* (New York, Columbia University Press).

Dube, M. (2009) 'I am because we are': giving primacy to African indigenous values in HIV&AIDS prevention, in: M. F. Murove (Ed.) *African ethics: an anthology of comparative and applied ethics* (Pietermaritzburg, South Africa, University of KwaZulu-Natal Press), 188–217.

Edwards, C. (1975) Societal complexity and moral development: a Kenyan study, *Ethos*, 3(4), 505–527.

Feltham, B. & Cottingham, J. (Eds) (2010) *Partiality and impartiality: morality, special relationships and the wider world* (Oxford, Oxford University Press).

Frankena, W. (1963) *Ethics* (Englewood Cliffs, NJ, Prentice-Hall).

Gaie, J. (2007) The Setswana concept of *Botho*: unpacking the metaphysical and moral aspects, in: J. Gaie & S. Mmolai (Eds) *The concept of Botho and HIV/AIDS in Botswana* (Eldoret, Kenya, Zapf Chancery), 29–43.

Gbadegesin, S. (1991) *African philosophy: traditional Yoruba philosophy and contemporary African realities* (New York, Peter Lang).

Grube, G. M. A. (Trans.) (1974) *Plato's Republic* (Indianapolis, Hackett).

Gyekye, K. (1997) *Tradition and modernity: philosophical reflections on the African experience* (New York, Oxford University Press).

Gyekye, K. (2004) *Beyond cultures: perceiving a common humanity* (Washington, DC, The Council for Research in Values and Philosophy).

Harding, S. (1987/1998) The curious coincidence of feminine and African moralities, in: E. C. Eze (Ed.) *African philosophy: an anthology* (Malden, MA, Blackwell), 360–372.

Harman, G. (1975) Moral relativism defended, *Philosophical Review*, 84(1), 3–22.

Ikuenobe, P. (2006) *Philosophical perspectives on communalism and morality in African traditions* (Lanham, MD, Rowman & Littlefield).

Iroegbu, P. (2005) Beginning, purpose and end of life, in: P. Iroegbu & A. Echekwube (Eds) *Kpim of morality ethics: general, special & professional* (Ibadan, Nigeria, Heinemann Educational Books), 440–445.

Irwin, T. (Trans.) (2000) *Aristotle: Nicomachean ethics* (2nd edn) (Indianapolis, Hackett).

Jeske, D. (2008) *Rationality and moral theory: how intimacy generates reasons* (New York, Routledge).

Kasenene, P. (1998) *Religious ethics in Africa* (Kampala, Uganda, Fountain Publishers).

Kasenene, P. (2000) African ethical theory and the four principles, in: R. M. Veatch (Ed.) *Cross-cultural perspectives in medical ethics* (Sudbury, MA, Jones and Bartlett), 347–357.

Kohlberg, L. (1976) Moral stages and moralization: the cognitive-developmental approach, in: T. Lickona (Ed.) *Moral development and behavior: theory, research, and social issues* (New York, Holt, Rinehart and Winston), 31–53.

Kohlberg, L. (1984) *The psychology of moral development* (San Francisco, Harper & Row).

Kohlberg, L. (1986) A current statement on some theoretical issues, in: S. Modgil & C. Modgil (Eds) *Lawrence Kohlberg: consensus and controversy* (London, The Falmer Press), 485–546.

Krog, A. (2008) 'This thing called reconciliation ...'; forgiveness as part of an interconnectedness-towards-wholeness, *South African Journal of Philosophy*, 27(4), 353–366.

Letseka, M. (2000) African philosophy and educational discourse, in: P. Higgs, N. C. G. Vakalisa, T. V. Mda & N. T. Assie-Lumumba (Eds) *African voices in education* (Cape Town, South Africa, Juta), 179–193.

Louw, D. (2006) The African concept of *Ubuntu* and restorative justice, in: D. Sullivan & L. Tifft (Eds) *Handbook of restorative justice: a global perspective* (New York, Routledge), 161–172.

Magesa, L. (1997) *African religion: the moral traditions of abundant life* (Maryknoll, NY, Orbis Books).

Masolo, D. A. (2004) Western and African communitarianism: a comparison, in: K. Wiredu (Ed.) *A companion to African philosophy* (Malden, MA, Blackwell), 483–497.

Mbiti, J. S. (1969) *African religions and philosophy* (London, Heinemann).

Menkiti, I. (2004) On the normative conception of a person, in: K. Wiredu (Ed.) *A companion to African philosophy* (Malden, MA, Blackwell), 324–331.

Metz, T. (2007) Toward an African moral theory, *Journal of Political Philosophy*, 15(3), 321–341.

Metz, T. (2010) Human dignity, capital punishment, and an African moral theory: toward a new philosophy of human rights, *Journal of Human Rights*, 9(1), 81–99.

Miller, R. (1992) *Moral differences* (Princeton, NJ, Princeton University Press).

Mkhize, N. (2008) *Ubuntu* and harmony: an African approach to morality and ethics, in: R. Nicolson (Ed.) *Persons in community: African ethics in a global culture* (Pietermaritzburg, South Africa, University of KwaZulu-Natal Press), 35–44.

Mokgoro, Y. (1998) *Ubuntu* and the law in South Africa, *Potchefstroom Electronic Law Journal*, 1(1), 15–26.

Murove, M. F. (2009) African bioethics: an exploratory discourse, in: M. F. Murove (Ed.) *African ethics: an anthology of comparative and applied ethics* (Pietermaritzburg, South Africa, University of KwaZulu-Natal Press), 157–177.

Noddings, N. (1984) *Caring: a feminine approach to ethics and moral education* (Berkeley, CA, University of California Press).

Noddings, N. (1992) *The challenge to care in schools* (New York, Teachers College Press).

Pearce, C. (1990) *Tsika, hunhu* and the moral education of primary school children, *Zambezia*, 17(2), 145–160.

Prinsloo, E. D. (1998) *Ubuntu* culture and participatory management, in: P. H. Coetzee & A. P. J. Roux (Eds) *Philosophy from Africa; a text with readings* (Cape Town, Oxford University Press Southern Africa), 41–51.

Ramose, M. (1999) *African philosophy through Ubuntu* (Harare, Mond Books).

Rawls, J. (1971) *A theory of justice* (Cambridge, MA, Harvard University Press).

Reed, D. C. (Ed.) (2008) Special Issue: towards an integrated model of moral functioning, *Journal of Moral Education*, 37(3), 279–428.

Sandel, M. (1984) The procedural republic and the unencumbered self, *Political Theory*, 12(1), 81–96.

Scheffler, S. (2001) *Boundaries and allegiances* (Oxford, Oxford University Press).

Setiloane, G. M. (1976) *The image of God among the Sotho-Tswana* (Rotterdam, Netherlands, Balkema).

Shutte, A. (2001) *Ubuntu: an ethic for the new South Africa* (Cape Town, South Africa, Cluster Publications).

Silberbauer, G. (1991) Ethics in small-scale societies, in: P. Singer (Ed.) *A companion to ethics* (Oxford, Basil Blackwell), 14–28.

Tutu, D. (1999) *No future without forgiveness* (New York, Random House).

Verhoef, H. & Michel, C. (1997) Studying morality within the African context: a model of moral analysis and construction, *Journal of Moral Education*, 26(4), 389–407.

Walzer, M. (1983) *Spheres of justice: a defense of pluralism and equality* (New York, Basic Books).

Williams, T. (Trans.) (1993) *Augustine: on free choice of the will* (Indianapolis, Hackett).

Wiredu, K. (1992a) The African concept of personhood, in: H. E. Flack & E. E. Pellegrino (Eds) *African-American perspectives on biomedical ethics* (Washington DC, Georgetown University Press), 104–117.

Wiredu, K. (1992b) The moral foundations of an African culture, in: K. Wiredu & K. Gyekye (Eds) *Person and community: Ghanaian philosophical studies, Volume 1* (Washington, DC, The Council for Research in Values and Philosophy), 193–206.

The death of democracy and the resurrection of timocracy

Mogobe B. Ramose

University of South Africa, South Africa

Throughout the centuries the ownership of wealth has been used as the measure for the determination of status in a community or society. Exactly what constituted wealth differed from one period to the next. The nature and extent of power within the narrow confines of the family and the wider political context was defined on the basis of ownership of wealth. Wealth power was transmuted into the authority to influence government and social morality. 'What I have' superseded 'I am a human being' and was thus decisive in the determination and adjudication of justice in human relations. This experience and concept of human relations in the sphere of politics was manifest in ancient Greece. It has persisted in different forms in the evolution of Western political philosophy and is an enduring reality of our time. Concretely, it left democracy intact only in name and replaced it with timocracy, or rule by money. This replacement is politically disturbing as it is a surreptitious negation of the principle of popular sovereignty. It is also morally disturbing because it undermines the principle of justice in human as well as in international politics. Accordingly, I explore the implications of this situation for moral education. The thesis defended in this paper is that the supersession of democracy by timocracy is ethically untenable. *Feta kgomo o tshware motho*—directly translated as 'go past the cow and catch the human being' is an ethical maxim in the African philosophy of *Ubuntu* among the Bantu-speaking peoples. It is a philosophy whose practice is opposed to this supersession of democracy by timocracy.

Introduction

The ethical question addressed in this essay is whether or not money, a human invention, should be permitted to retain its sovereignty over all spheres of human life. At issue is not only the sovereignty of money but, more fundamentally, the subordination of the dignity of the human person to money. The sovereignty of money has crystallised into the idea that individual, and sometimes group, authority to create and adjudicate upon communal and social morality derives from the ownership of wealth. Thus the ownership of wealth is constituted into the foundation of justice in human relations in general and particularly in politics. In this situation, justice is the servant of the ownership of wealth. Accordingly, it loses its character and core as the measure and guardian of the principle of equality among human beings. Like equality, justice is an empty concept to be filled in substantively and constantly according to the imperatives of the evolving human condition. The death of democracy and its surreptitious substitution by timocracy (rule by money) reinstates in our time the question of justice in human relations both within the state and in the broader context of international politics.

Consequently, this essay traces the origins of this problematic from ancient Greece and its evolution until the contemporary period. However, this is not to say that I claim to be pursuing a historical study of the problem. Rather I give an outline of the main features and points of connection illustrating how the problem spread globally from ancient Greece to our contemporary period. Colonisation and decolonisation are crucial links in the spread of Western democracy and timocracy to many regions of the world. Thus the problem here is not just about Africa but about the wider world of international politics that we live in today. In general, the grant of independence at decolonisation was virtually restricted to the political domain. It left the erstwhile coloniser in effective control over the economy of the decolonised (Easterly, 2006).

Furthermore, the famous saying of Aristotle that 'man is a rational animal' played a role, inadvertently, in the subordination of the woman, especially in her capacity as a wife, to the money of her husband. According to Lange (1983) it implied that 'woman is not a rational animal'. Through their debate on whether or not it is the man or the woman who imparts life to the foetus, Plato and Aristotle further contributed in very large measure to the idea that the woman is by 'nature' inferior to the man (Dickanson, 1976; Gould, 1976; Spelman, 1983). This valuation of the woman had an impact on the participation of the woman in communal and social affairs. In practice it meant that the woman was subordinated to the will of the man. Among others, the subordination confined the woman to domestic affairs and effectively denied her the opportunity to acquire economic power in her own right. Ancient Roman law upheld this subordination through the principle and practice of *pater familias* (interpreted as 'the father as head of the family'). The modern law of husband and wife metamorphosed the *pater familias* by inventing 'marital power', which could be waived only through an ante-nuptial contract. The common thread running through all this is that the woman was, to all intents and purposes, an appendage of the man; a veritable 'dependant' along with children. The basis for the inequality between man and woman was not 'nature' but culture defined primarily by wealth. The wealth owned by the man thus determined and defined his putative superiority over the woman. Her dependency was cultivated by culture and institutionalised by law. In this we see within the narrow confines of the family the operation of the idea that the ownership of wealth determines and defines power.

This idea was extended to the wider sphere of politics. During the time of the French Revolution it was noted that 'the liberty, equality and fraternity' espoused by French revolutionaries was meant for men only and was subsequently questioned[1] (Riemer & Fout, 1983). The ban on women's participation in politics through the exercise of the right to vote was lifted relatively recently even in so-called mature democracies (Ray, 1919). The right to vote was frequently qualified by property ownership, which more often than not excluded women. Money, therefore, seems to also lie at the heart of the contemporary struggle for the emancipation of the woman.

In what follows, I outline the evolution of the experience and concept that the ownership of wealth (money) determines and defines power and authority in human relations. I suggest that even during the life time of Jesus, money was a threat to the moral fabric of society, just as it was in ancient Greece. I then turn to consider the farewell speech of United States of America President Eisenhower (1961) and argue that it offers a landmark statement ushering in the contemporary period of timocracy. It is the speech of an insider highlighting a specific insight from the experience of government. It also offers an invitation to the philosopher to critically examine this insight.

I argue that timocracy may not prevail over democracy since the latter is the means to establish, protect and preserve justice in human relations. The Sesotho—one of the Bantu languages—proverb of *feta kgomo o tshware motho*, translated literally as 'go past the cow and catch the human being' means that if you are faced with the dilemma to make a decisive choice between the protection of wealth (the cow) and the preservation of human life then you are obliged to opt for the latter. I will use this proverb to anchor and support the argument that it is unethical for timocracy to supersede democracy. In addition, the theory and practice of 'development' will be used as one of the examples in support of my argument. Finally, I will illustrate the relevance of this argument to moral education. I begin by describing and defining timocracy specifically as it is one of the key terms in this essay.

The meaning of timocracy

The *Oxford English Dictionary* (2010) defines timocracy in two ways: according to Aristotle as 'A polity with a property qualification for the ruling class'; and, according to Plato, as 'A polity (like that of Sparta) in which love of honour is said to be the dominant motive with the rulers'. Wikipedia (2010) explains timocracy as 'A form of government in which civic honour or political power increases with the amount of property one owns' or 'A form of government in which ambition for honour, power and military glory motivates the rulers'. For this purpose, I adopt here the meaning of timocracy to be that 'property' or wealth determines and defines the nature and extent of political power. Because of the centrality of money in the creation and accumulation of wealth, I adapt this understanding and construe timocracy as a money-based form of government or, more colloquially, the rule by money.

Timocracy in ancient Greece

Democracy in the evolution of Western political philosophy is one among many attempts to give meaning and content to the concept of justice. Over time, democracy, anchored in the separation of governmental powers and reinforced by a Bill of Rights, came to be recognised as the guarantor and defender of justice in politics.

This appears as a quantum leap from the time of Solon, the sixth century BC lawgiver of ancient Greece, who provided Athens with a constitution which introduced the ideas of timocracy (or *timokratia*) as a graded oligarchy (Stanton, 1990). Solon, in defining four tiers[2] of the population according to the amount each man produced in a year, and relating such production to political rights, can be said to have instituted the first form of timocracy. Underlying Solon's definition and classification of the four tiers of the population in a timocracy is the regulative idea that ownership of wealth defines and determines communal status and, by extension, the exercise of power and authority in a community and society. Solon's timocracy undermines the principle of equality among human beings. Accordingly, it compromises justice because power is concentrated with those who are the owners of wealth. Consequently, the potential for corruption and the violation of natural rights are both high. The argument of the present essay is that the 'potential' referred to above is, to all intents and purposes, an illustration of how timocracy undermines justice in human relations. This calls for a challenge intended to stop the violation of the 'natural rights' of human beings.

The age of money

This sub-heading does not purport to answer the question: 'how old is money?' Instead, it is intended to focus more upon a period of time. Ancient Greece provides an opportunity to explore the meaning and impact of money in the conduct of human relations. Although Solon gave ancient Athens a timocratic constitution, he certainly had reservations about wealth and money in the conduct of politics. According to Seaford (2004), a classical scholar, Solon writes thus of the phenomenon of money; 'Of wealth there is no limit that appears to men. For those of us who have the most wealth are eager to double it' (pp. 165–166). Erotic passion for money is also inscribed in an anonymous fragment cited by Seaford: 'O gold, offspring of the earth, what passion…you kindle among humankind, mightiest of all, tyrant over all' (p. 172). Furthermore, the proverb '[It is gold and silver] by which war and the other things…thrive' (pp. 164–165) may be construed as an ironic prophecy of Judas Iscariot's betrayal of Jesus just for 30 pieces of silver as recorded in John 13:21–30, Luke 22:1–6, and Mark 14:12–21 of *The Holy Bible* (New King James, 1982). The betrayal is somewhat hurtful to moral sensitivity. The hurt is so deep that for Mark, the Gospel writer, it would have been much better for the betrayer not to have been born at all than to be born and commit the act of betrayal.

The above insights about money were already deeply rooted in ancient Greek culture long before Greek philosophers Plato (born in Athens in 428 BC) and Aristotle (384–322 BC) espoused their philosophies on timocracy. It is somewhat curious that Protagoras of Abdera in Thrace (481 BC) in ancient Greece, found it fitting to espouse his epistemology on the famous premise that 'man is the measure of all things, of those that are, that they are, of those that are not, that they are not' (quoted in Copleston, 1962, p. 108), apparently oblivious of the deep-rooted culture of money in his time.

It was this cultural climate that Solon was upon called to resolve. His resolution was the provision of the constitution for Athens based upon the insistence that there must be limits to the desirability of wealth and its power (Seaford, 2004). Through the ethics contained in his poetry, Solon urged his fellow citizens embrace moderation in their ambitions and intentions. And long after Solon, Aristotle, soaked in Greek culture, would reaffirm moderation in the elaboration of his eudaemonistic ethics (with happiness as its goal) espoused in the *Nichomachean ethics* (Stumpf & Fieser, 2002).

Morality and education

Aristotle's idea that happiness is the end or purpose of all human conduct does have implications for moral education. Education, understood as a guide and nurturing of the quest for happiness, involves first the home and then the school or university where it is formal. The two domains of learning are not mutually exclusive. On the contrary, they are, ideally, complementary. Education should focus on guiding the learner to attain happiness, both in the learning process itself and in the future once formal learning has ended. But today one can hardly speak of the end of formal learning since learning must be viewed as a lifelong project.

The idea of lifelong learning is consistent with the quest for truth as one of the basic aims of education. Truth is not known once and for all. It is to be searched for constantly in the ever-changing situations of the human condition. The knowledge of truth is to be shared through and with others as no single individual can be the sole and authoritative repository of truth. The existential necessity to search for knowledge through and with others and to disseminate it imposes the need to recognise the human dignity of one another. The search for truth and knowledge is about the meaning of life. Ultimately, it is about the meaning of the human person. Herein lies the ethical dimension to education (Pope John Paul II, 1990). This by itself entails the obligation to recognise and respect the limits of our freedom in human relations. Thus the virtue of moderation becomes the thread that weaves and binds human relations into a continually unfolding oneness.

Human relations based on the recognition, respect and protection of the human dignity of one another require moral education that is focused upon the integral development of the individual and oriented to community service. Such education is ethically significant since it answers to the individual need to have access to as well as to use the resources necessary for the preservation of life. Thus the question of justice arises in the sense of giving the other their due. It also arises in the sense of distributive justice. It is justice that imposes limits upon the quest for individual happiness. It enjoins individuals to exercise moderation in accumulating and allocating to themselves the necessities of life. Moral education should cultivate these insights in the learner. It can do so by adopting a holistic approach to formal education enabling the learner to understand that education is not for self-edification only and always in relation to the others. There is thus a link between morality and education.

The connection between morality and education is challenged from many angles today. The challenge requires that university teachers:

> should seek to improve their competence and endeavour to set the content, objectives, methods, and results of research in an individual discipline within the framework of a coherent world vision....All teachers are to be inspired by academic ideals and by the principles of an authentically human life. Students are challenged to pursue an education that combines excellence in humanistic and cultural development with specialized professional training. Most especially, they are challenged to continue the search for truth and for meaning throughout their lives. (Pope John Paul II, 1990, para. 22 and 23)

The theory and practice of development

The theory and practice of 'development' constitutes one illustration of the prominence of timocracy. One of the major problems pertaining to development aid is the fact that the poor have no significant voice and role with regard to the acquisition and utilisation of such aid (Hancock, 1989; Easterly, 2006). Moyo (2009) also decries Africa's dependency on aid and censures the fact that the poor do not have a real voice in the 'debate on an exit strategy from the aid quagmire' (p. 67). The absence of political voice due to lack of money means that money is central to development, to the extent that it determines who may live or die.

In view of the deadly effects of development aid on the one hand and its apparent failure to lift the poor out of the bondage of economic dependency on the other, the question is whether or not such aid should be continued. For Hancock (1989) the answer is that 'the lords of poverty must depart' (p. 193).

While some espouse 'good governance' as a condition of aid, good governance does not necessarily strengthen democracy, nor does it eliminate corruption (Easterly, 2006, p. 129). Rather, money is the means of corruption and corruption sub-serves the purpose of accumulating more money. It has the ability to undermine democracy and make it stand only as an empty shell. As international philanthropist, George Soros (1998), comments:

> There has always been corruption, but in the past people were ashamed of it and tried to hide it. Now that the profit motive has been promoted into a moral principle, politicians in some countries feel ashamed when they fail to take advantage of their position. (p. 204)

This elevation of the profit motive to a moral principle, Soros argues, is anchored in the ideology of competition.

The elevation of the profit motive to a moral principle is even more disturbing when it finds support from philosophers. According to Presby (2002), 'philosophers like Ayn Rand and Garrett Hardin provided the ideology for the actions of Reagan–Thatcher economists, who suggested that the poor must rather starve and die than become perennial charity cases for those who have riches' (p. 286). The sentencing of the poor to death is consistent with the ideology of competition. It is, however, contrary to the original meaning of competition. Etymologically, competition means the common pursuit of a common goal (Arnsperger, 1996). It means—*cum petere*—to seek together the best solution to the right problem in the right place and at the right time. It means the selection of the best is not reduced to the unique (Group of Lisbon, 1995). Whereas in this original meaning competition recognises the 'other' and embraces the 'other' as a cooperative pursuer of a common goal, in its contemporary meaning it is the exclusion of the 'other'. Ontologically, it is tantamount to denying the existence of the 'other' and thus expressive of the willingness to kill the 'other'. Contemporary competition thus proceeds from the metaphysical premise that thou shalt kill another human being in order to survive. The killing is both literal and metaphorical (Arnsperger, 1996).

This metaphysics of killing in the name of competition means that in our time the survival of the fittest through the acquisition and possession of money is the goal of human existence. The pursuit of this goal entails the replacement of democracy with timocracy. The replacement is an urgent moral challenge that demands an answer. The challenge is not limited to teachers and students. It faces entire communities, locally and globally. Moral education today must cultivate the sensitivity of learners to such problems and make them understand that it is their task to seek, not any answer, but the answer that is truthful and faithful to the exigency to recognise, respect and protect the human dignity of everyone on planet Earth.

I concur with Soros (1998) that the starting point for the reinvention of social values in our time is that there ought to be more to life than mere survival. An integral part of this starting point is that the elevation of the profit motive into an ethical principle is an aberration. Therefore, money may not be the measure of all things.

Democracy and the legitimacy of government

Philosophers like Aristotle, Jean Jacques Rousseau, John Locke and Thomas Hobbes have espoused different versions of democracy. Despite the differences in time, perspective and emphasis, what is discernable is that democracy involves the voluntary renunciation by the individual of the right to use violence only on condition that others are willing to do the same. In effect the state in the form of the government is vested with the sole and exclusive power to use and control violence. The government's monopoly over the use and control of armed force may not be arbitrary and unlimited. The government is obliged to account to its citizens for resort to the use of violence. Accountability is a vital ingredient of democracy since the state, in the first place, owes its conditional existence to the voluntary consent of its citizenry. Without accountability to its citizenry the state loses its legitimacy (O'Brien & Shannon, 1995, p. 18).

It is my contention that timocracy in our time has undermined the legitimacy of government. It is a challenge to the citizens to 'repudiate' and rethink the state. I now turn to elaborate upon this contention.

The military-industrial complex—the age of timocracy

Forty-eight years ago, President Eisenhower of the United States of America inaugurated the contemporary age of timocracy in his famous farewell speech of

17 January 1961 (Eisenhower, 1961). As already stated, the experience and insight, especially of the insider, is the point of departure for philosophical analysis. A cursory observation of contemporary domestic and international politics reveals the extent to which the President's speech is both relevant to and true of our time. The outgoing President declared that 'in the councils of government, we must guard against the acquisition of unwarranted influence, whether sought or unsought, by the military industrial complex. The potential for the disastrous rise of misplaced power exists and will persist' (LaFeber, 1973, quoted in Eisenhower, 1961, pp. 646–647).

There is no doubt that the President's warning was based on experience, knowledge and insight into the operations of government. If it is eventually acquired, the influence of the military–industrial complex (MIC) would be 'unwarranted' because it would be devoid of the will of the people. Accordingly, it would have no mandate to replace a democratically elected government or contend with it over the exercise of governmental power. It would simply be an illegitimate source of governmental power contradicting and undermining the principle of popular sovereignty. As such the 'unwarranted' influence would also dispense with the vital ingredient of accountability to the citizenry. The influence would indeed be 'misplaced' because it would just be an inappropriate misfit in the structure of government. It would be 'disastrous' because its primary motive force would be the protection and promotion of its own interest, namely, the pursuit of wealth or money making (Singer 2003, p. 64).

Pilger (2002) too, responds to the President's speech and, by extension, questions Singer's interpretation thereof. He avers that:

> the widely held belief among anti-globalisation campaigners that the state has 'withered away' is misguided, along with the view that transnational corporate power has replaced the state and, by extension, imperialism...[quoting Kagarlitsky] 'globalisation does not mean the impotence of the state, but the rejection by the state of its social functions, in favour of repressive ones, and the ending of democratic freedoms'. (p. 5)

Whenever the state attacks the rights of its citizenry it risks the dissolution of the common wealth. The risk is precisely the renunciation of the principle of popular sovereignty and the obligation to recognise, protect and promote the rights of the citizens. The actualisation of this risk can ultimately lead to the 'withering away' of the state, that is, the literal change of government. According to Singer (2003, pp. 60–61), Pilger's claim that 'transnational corporate power' has not replaced the state is unsustainable. Furthermore, Pilger's claim appears to overlook the widespread proliferation of questionable arms deals such as Bofors (India), Agusta (Belgium), Al Yamamah (Saudi Arabia) and Schabir Schaik (South Africa). This proliferation speaks to the penetration of the unwarranted and palpable influence of the MIC over government. With regard to South Africa, Feinstein (2007) notes that 'The South African Parliament of today, elected by all the country's people, is an empty vessel. The majority of its members provide little or no oversight of the Executive, who in turn pay it minimal heed' (p. 240). And this observation harmonises with a similar one referring to the USA that has to do with the hiring of a multitude of privatised military forces (PMFs) beginning in the second term of the Clinton administration:

The United States quietly arranged the hire of...[PMFs] whose operations...range far beyond the narrow restrictions placed on US soldiers fighting the drug war....The extensive PMF involvement in the war in Colombia and its neighbouring states by US-based firms has been entirely without Congressional notification, oversight, or approval....Such marginalization of the legislature is a contravention of the role the Founding Fathers intended for Congress in the Constitution. The legislature was intended to be equal to the other branches and to provide the democratic voice of the citizenry in shaping policy. (Singer, 2003, pp. 207, 209 and 215)

This unfolding reality confirms the fears of President Eisenhower and illustrates the vacuity of Pilger's claim.

The resurrection of timocracy

The end of the Cold War further paved the way for the rise of PMFs (Singer, 2003). The existence of PMFs is a solidly entrenched practice in the United States of America and beyond. Faced with demobilised and unemployed soldiers as part of the transition to the new constitutional dispensation, South Africa tacitly approved PMF operations outside its boundaries (Singer, 2003). This was an alternative to the dangerous situation of keeping highly skilled soldiers idle. It was probably also an inadvertent acknowledgement that the PMF phenomenon had already penetrated South Africa (Feinstein, 2007, p. 245).

The PMF phenomenon is a practice that has potentially disastrous implications for democracy. Among these, Singer (2003) points out the following: abdication of responsibility by government; an undermined social contract between government and citizenry; weakened citizen loyalty; and the contested legitimacy of a regime. 'Politics are now directly and openly linked with economic interests (in normative terms, a return to a timocratic or money-based system of governance), which can lead to breakdown of respect for governmental authority, and also delegitimizes its right to rule' (p. 206).

And so it is that over a long historical trajectory we have returned back to timocracy. Just as Solon responded to the injustice and destruction of the unbridled pursuit of wealth during his time, so are we challenged to answer to the morally untenable and the politically unwarranted substitution of democracy with timocracy. My response to this challenge is to search for an answer from the wisdom of African philosophy.[3]

Wisdom from African philosophy

A proverb provides the first response to the challenge of timocracy. The Sesotho proverb *Le bona tsa bopudi kgakala, tsa bonku di bipilwe ke mesela*, translated as 'the backside of the goat is open to view whereas that of the sheep is covered by its tail', speaks to the question of communal justice. It is couched in polite but subtle language referring to the comparative visibility of the private parts of goats and sheep. It avers that with some effort one can eventually see the private parts of a goat. However those of a sheep cannot be seen because they are covered by its wide and large tail. This is a metaphorical expression meaning that justice for the poor is difficult to realise, whereas it is often accessible to and by the wealthy. Here we notice that even in African philosophy, the experience and concept that wealth determines and defines the communal status of individuals existed. The nature and extent of individual authority and exertion of influence in communal affairs was anchored upon the individual's ownership of wealth. The injustice arising from this philopraxis was recognised. It undermined the principle of human equality expressed in the ethical maxim that *motho ke motho ka batho*—a human being acquires humanness through and together with other human beings. This called for a remedy restoring the principle of human equality.

The concept of community in the African philosophy of *Ubuntu* (*Botho*—*humanness*) is comprised of three tiers, namely, the living, the living-dead ('ancestors') and the yet to be born. Life is salubrious and just if harmony prevails in these tiers of community. 'For Black Africa, it is not the Cartesian *cogito ergo sum* but an existential *cognatus sum, ergo sumus* [I am related, therefore we are] that is decisive' (Bujo, 2001, p. 22). The point here is that, in contrast to the assertion of the French philosopher, Rene Descartes, 'I think, therefore, I exist' emphasising the 'I', the philosophical perspective of 'I am related, therefore we are' emphasises the 'we'. These contrasting philosophical perspectives do have the potential for different practical consequences in the sphere of human relations.

The living-dead play a vital role in the life of the living as they are deemed to have special powers the living do not have. Because of this belief it is crucial to be attentive to their 'whisper' and carry out the wishes or instructions received. The carrying out of the instructions is understood to be obligatory on the premise that the living-dead are the protectors of the life of the living and as such wish them only the good. Congolese philosopher, Bénézet Bujo (1997) explains:

> If attention were genuinely paid to the innovative elements in African tradition, it would scarcely be possible for dictatorship—so common in the black continent—to exist, since oppression in all its forms is incompatible with the anamnetic solidarity which recalls the duty of continually realizing the three dimensional fellowship anew....Within a tradition understood in this way, it is never permissible to infringe human rights....[and] includes equally the injustice done to those who lived in the past. This naturally also involves the guilt of the ancestors; solidarity requires that this be expiated by their descendants. (p. 72)

The living-dead belong to the lineage of a particular extended family. One cannot invoke the living-dead of another family to seek protection and succour from them. This limitation does not preclude the possibility and, indeed, the reality of access to justice in the communal context. The communal structure of relations is permeated by the ethical maxim that *motho ke motho ka batho* (humanity is achieved through others). This enjoins everyone to remain a human being, that is, to recognise, respect and protect the humanness of the other humans. Only in this way does one ensure that one does not denigrate to the status of *selo*, that is, a thing, a non-human being. Thus *Ubuntu* (*Botho*) is the measure of one's own humanness. On this reasoning, *motho* without *botho* is a contradiction in terms. The vital point here is that regardless of whatever possessions or wealth one might have, the first and fundamental point to recognise is that one is a human being and this status is preserved in relations with other human beings. This exclusion of wealth from the determination and definition of one as a human being forms the basis for yet another ethical maxim, namely, *feta kgomo o tshware motho*. This means that if one is faced with the dilemma of choosing between the protection of wealth and the preservation of human life then one must opt for the latter. It is the actualisation of this maxim in practice that I maintain will be the antithesis to the timocracy that has now superseded democracy in our time.

Conclusion

The practice of *feta kgomo o tshware motho* requires moral education based upon the principles of sharing, concern and care for one another and the subordination of wealth to the dignity of the human person as *motho*. It is a philosophical practice that exists in day to day life in both urban and rural South Africa among the African peoples. For example, being a passenger in a non-metered taxi requires a lot of *Ubuntu/Botho*. First, one must have patience because the taxi will not move until it is full. But a full taxi does not always mean carrying the correct number of legally prescribed passengers. Where a seat is for three passengers, the driver may easily demand that it be occupied by four. So, one requires tolerance in addition to patience. It is of, course, clear that one may object and even educate the driver that overloading the vehicle is illegal.

This course of action is, however, not advisable. For one thing, the provisions of the law do not appear to be considered seriously by both the driver and other passengers: one of the arguments may be that it is important to show concern and care for others who also would like to arrive at work on time or reach home while it is safe in the streets. This apparently spurious reason can actually assume greater significance when the taxi driver deviates from the normal route in order to help one or more passengers to reach their workplace on time. In the evenings, the taxi may also follow too many routes just in order to put the female passengers closer to their destination. All this does not show that the driver and the passengers appreciate that the fare paid becomes much less and therefore less profitable than the service rendered. Yet, the point is that it is not the fare—the money—that matters first but the care and concern for another human being. This is the picture I draw from an analysis of the situation and the conversations that go on in the taxis. It does not mean, however, that all is smooth. Some of the objections I have indicated are treated with contempt and, sometimes even with violence. It is a complex situation that illustrates the ensuing tension between the contending values in South African society. It is the task of moral education to be aware of this tension and to provide a resolution that preserves and protects human dignity.

In rural South Africa and, to some extent in the urban areas as well, it is not unusual to find neighbours helping one another with food or even coal or some other fuel to make fire for cooking. This is not common practice among those brought up under the 'I' philosophical orientation to life. In both the urban and rural areas, attending the funerals of neighbours is regarded as an important expression of *Ubuntu* in the sharing of grief, assisting and consoling the bereaved as an expression of care and concern about them. If one does not take this seriously, when death visits their family they are simply left alone. But funerals tend to be rather private affairs for those brought up under the 'I' philosophical perspective. Although one orientation is not necessarily superior or better than another, the point is that they tend to clash when their respective adherents interact. Again moral education is called upon to impress upon us the importance of patience with one another and the necessity for dialogue aimed at the betterment of mutual understanding.

Finally, the larger part of the population in South Africa is rural. It is not over-whelmed by Westernisation as the urban *motho* generally is. *Feta kgomo o tshware motho* is the living philosophical practice of the majority of rural dwellers and some living in the urban areas. The point of this observation is that this integral aspect of *Ubuntu* philosophy is still alive. For those wedded to the 'I' philosophy, time is money and the invitation to patience might just require some adaptation. It will require appreciating in practice the fact that money may not take precedence over the preservation and protection of human life. The acceptance of this perspective would constitute an advance in the struggle against timocracy today.

Notes

1. Upon the realisation of this state of affairs, Olympe de Gouges (1748–1793) published 'The Declaration of the rights of women' in 1790, modelled on the 'Declaration of the Rights of Man and the Citizen' of 1789 in France (Riemer & Fout, 1983).
2. These were the Pentacosiomedimni, men who produced 500 bushels, could serve as generals in the army; the Hippeis or Knights, produced 300 bushels a year and could maintain them-selves and one horse for war; the Zeugitae or Tillers, who produced 200 bushels a year and owned at least two beasts of burden; and the Thetes or manual labourers who produced nothing. The Thetes were excluded from office, while only the Pentacosiomedimni could hold high office (Stanton, 1990).
3. The question whether or not African philosophy exists persists. The curious point about it is that similar expressions such as Indian, Russian, Japanese, Chinese or American philosophy or even Western philosophy do not invite the question whether or not such philosophies exist. The core of the question ultimately bears on whether or not Africans are members of the 'rational animal' group. This notwithstanding, the present writer affirms the existence of African philosophy both in terms of the etymological meaning of philosophy as the love of wisdom and philosophy as an academic discipline. On this basis, the present writer shall proceed to consider a response to the challenge of timocracy.

References

Arnsperger, C. (1996) *Competition, consumerism and the 'other': a philosophical investigation into the ethics of economic competition* (Louvain-La-Neuve, Belgium, Institut de Recherches Economiques, Université Catholique de Louvain).

Bujo, B. (1997) *The ethical dimension of community: the African model and the dialogue between North and South* (Nairobi, Kenya, Paulines Publications Africa).

Bujo, B. (2001) *Foundations of an African ethic* (New York, Crosswood Publishing Company).

Copleston, F. (1962) *A history of philosophy* (New York, Doubleday & Company).

Dickanson, A. (1976) Anatomy and destiny: the role of biology in Plato's views of women, in: C. Gould & M.W. Wartofsky (Eds) *Women and philosophy* (New York, G.P. Putnam's Sons), 45–53.

Easterly, W. (2006) *The white man's burden: why the West's efforts to aid the rest have done so much ill and so little good* (New York, Penguin Group).

Eisenhower, D. D. (1961) *Farewell address by President Dwight D. Eisenhower. Final TV Talk 1/17/ 61 (1), Box 38, Speech Series. Papers of Dwight D. Eisenhower as President, 1953-61* (Abilene, KS, USA, Eisenhower Library, National Archives and Records Administration).

Feinstein, A. (2007) *After the party* (Cape Town, South Africa, Jonathan Ball).

Gould, C. (1976) The woman question: philosophy of liberation and the liberation of philosophy, in: C. Gould & M. W. Wartofsky (Eds) *Women and philosophy* (New York, G. P. Putnam's Sons).

Group of Lisbon (1995) *Limits to competition* (Cambridge, MA, MIT Press).

Hancock, G. (1989) *Lords of poverty* (Nairobi, Kenya, Camerapix International Publishers).

LaFeber, W. E. (Ed.) (1973) *Eastern Europe and the Soviet Union* (New York, Chelsea Publishers).

Lange, L. (1983) Woman is not a rational animal: on Aristotle's biology of reproduction, in: S. Harding & M. B. Hintikka (Eds) *Discovering reality* (Dordrecht, Germany, D. Reidel Publishing Company), 1–15.

Moyo, D. (2009) *Dead aid, why aid is not working and how there is another way for Africa* (London, Penguin Books).

New King James (1982) *The Holy Bible* (Nashville, TN, Thomas Nelson).

O'Brien, D. J. & Shannon, T. A. (Eds.) (1995) *Catholic social thought: the documentary heritage* (Maryknoll, NY, Orbis Books).

Oxford English Dictionary. (2010) *Timocracy*. Available online at: http://dictionary.oed.com/cgi/ entry/50252938?single=1&query_type=word&queryword=timocracy&first=1&max_to_ show=10 (accessed 20 April 2010).

Pilger, J. (2002) *The new rulers of the world* (London, Verso).

Pope John Paul II. (1990) *Ex corde ecclesiae: apostolic constitution of the Supreme Pontiff John Paul II on Catholic universities* (St Peter's, Vatican City).

Presby, G. M. (2002) African philosophers on global wealth distribution in: G. Presby, M. D. Smith, P. A. Abuya & O. Nyarwath (Eds) *Thought and practice in African philosophy: sixth annual conference of the International Society for African Philosophy and Studies* (Kenya, Nairobi, Konrad Adenauer Foundation).

Ray, P. O. (1919) The world-wide suffrage movement, *Journal of Comparative Legislation and International Law*, 1(1), 220–238.

Riemer, E. S. & Fout, J. C. (Eds) (1983) *European women: a documentary history, 1789–1945* (Brighton, UK, Harvester Press).

Seaford, R. (2004) *Money and the early Greek mind* (Cambridge, Cambridge University Press).

Singer, P. W. (2003) *Corporate warriors, the rise of the privatized military industry* (London, Cornell University Press).

Soros, G. (1998) *The crisis of global capitalism* (London, Little, Brown and Company).

Spelman, E. V. (1983) Aristotle and the politicization of the soul, in: S. Harding & M. B. Hintikka (Eds) *Discovering reality* (Dordrecht, Germany, D. Reidel Publishing Company), 17–30.

Stanton, G. R. (1990) *Athenian politics c800–500 BC: a sourcebook* (London, Routledge).

Stumpf, S. E. & Fieser, J. (2002) *Philosophy, history and problems* (Boston, MA, McGraw-Hill).

Wikipedia (2010) *Timocracy*. Available online at http://en.wikipedia.org/wiki/Timocracy (accessed 30 June 2009).

'Moral ecology' and 'moral capital': tools towards a sociology of moral education from a South African ethnography

Sharlene Swartz

Human Sciences Research Council, South Africa

Research and pedagogy in the field of morality and moral education has long been dominated by philosophical and psychological disciplines. Although sociological studies and theorising in the field have not been absent, it has been limited and non-systematic. Drawing on a study that investigated the lived morality of a group of young South Africans growing up in the aftermath of Apartheid and in the townships of Cape Town, this paper surveys the historical contribution made by sociologists to the study of morality and introduces two sociological notions of importance to moral education research and practice: 'moral ecology' and 'moral capital'. Employing Bronfenbrenner's ecological systems theory it describes the moral life as an ecology of interconnecting systems, complex antinomies, diverse codes, multiple positionings, discordant processes and competing influences, over time and on multiple levels. Moral capital, draws on Bourdieu's work on capitals and is described in two ways. First, as a dialectic, such that young people living in poverty identify how being 'good' can be translated into economic capital, which in turn enables them to remain 'good'. Second, it asks, what are the necessary elements of moral capital that young people need in order to be good and so attain the economic future to which they aspire? The paper concludes by noting how a sociology of moral education contributes to understanding the relationship between poverty and morality, including the social reproduction of morality; and its relevance for moral education research and practice.

Introduction

How do poor young people who live in impoverished communities develop moral lives? What difference does poor schooling, partial-parenting, a history of dehumanising racial subjugation and the normalisation of violence make to their lived morality? How do they retain their humanity in the midst of filthy environments, struggles for survival, the physiological effects of poverty, the absence of recreation and the widespread availability of alcohol and drugs? What tools are there to help us to consider their moral lives beyond linear developmental stages, middle-class definitions of the good life and short-sighted talk of moral choices? These are just some of the formative sociological questions that need to be asked of moral education in impoverished contexts. In order to answer them satisfactorily it is critical to consider what sociological theorising has been done on the topic of morality and moral education and then to explore how some of sociology's insights may best be applied to moral education research and practice.

The sociology of morality

Sociology is concerned with the study of society, human social interaction and the rules and processes that bind and separate people as members of associations, groups and institutions. It is materially interested in the way political, economic and social context affect human social functioning (Bourdieu *et al.*, 1991; Giddens & Birdsall, 2001). More specifically, the sociology of education is concerned with how public institutions affect education and its outcome, including the manner in which school-ing reproduces or perpetuates social class, inequalities and injustices (Bourdieu, 1997; Lauder, 2006).

Historically, sociologists have paid sporadic theoretical attention to the phenomena of human morality. In the nineteenth century, Emile Durkheim (1973a, 1973b), writ-ing in the context of the social and moral crisis following the dictatorship of the Third Napoleonic Republic, understood *society* as the source of morality that begins 'with attachment to something other than ourselves' (Durkheim, 1973b, p. 151). Georg Simmel (1950) held to similar ideas and spoke of the individual being confronted by a 'second subject' and of morality as social norms internalised by individuals that act as a 'collective conscience'. Durkheim further advocated that moral growth could be formally nurtured in schools through focusing on discipline, altruism, the importance of collective interest and 'sacrifice' (Durkheim, 1973b, p. 152). His suggested pedagogy was one which produced a 'critical consciousness' in which justice was paramount, rather than based on moral maxims (p. xi). He further believed that morality was a social fact that needed to be investigated 'attentively' (p. xv). Max Weber (1978, 2002), in contrast, argued for a distinction between facts and values. He saw social life as governed primarily by rational interest (capital) while acknowl-edging the existence of value-rational action—action shaped by commitment to a value that itself could not be rationally arrived at. He concluded that since morality primarily concerned self-interest, the individual was the sole moral authority (Thiele, 1996, p. 7). Other nineteenth-century sociologists, such as Karl Marx (1988), warned that morality is the convention of the ruling classes and is inherently about power, control and subjugation and ought to be viewed with suspicion.

In the twentieth century, important sociologists have commented on human morality, but still in limited rather than systematic fashion. For example, Zygmunt Bauman (1993) and Emmanuel Levinas (1987), largely reflecting Durkheim and Simmel, conclude that moral actions are not driven by normative theories, such as utilitarianism or deontology, but rather by localised and interpersonal relationships—through 'being for the other' (Levinas) or 'the moral party of two' (Bauman). Jürgen Habermas's (1990) concepts of 'communicative rationality' and 'discourse ethics' (p. 246) have contributed to moral pedagogy through his insistence that universalisable morality is arrived at by rational discussion within a community of solidarity. Thomas Luckmann (1983) draws attention to the importance of institutional environments with *contradictory* normative requirements and advocates a study of moral concepts (the way in which they are produced and can be negotiated) through the observation and analysis of everyday life or 'lifeworlds'. Michel Foucault (2000) extends Marx's 'power' analysis by showing how morality (and talk about morality) has been used in order to control people ideologically and socially. Other sociological contributions to moral theorising include functionalism (Parsons, 1937), sociobiology (Wilson, 1975) and rational choice theory (Abell, 1991).

More recently, a number of *empirical* projects have contributed to a sociological understanding of morality. Robert Bellah's (1996) study of the increasing individualisation of American society and its implications for civic life and human morality adds the notion of 'therapeutic contractualism' (p. 129) to the sociology of morality lexicon. People treat others based, not upon a concern for right or wrong, but rather upon care for others within an immediate circle of concern (p. 112) and with regard to 'what works for me' (p. 129). Other empirical sociological studies include Suttles's (1968) study dealing with the 'social order' and 'provincial morality' of slum neighbourhoods; Baumgartner's (1988) *The moral order of a suburb* and Anderson's (1999) *Code of the street*, looking at the 'moral life of the inner city'. Furthermore, economic sociologists have paid attention to the role moral values play in the marketplace (for example, Granovetter & Swedberg, 2001) and, more theoretically, Fein (1997) elucidates the informal social rules that people create in making moral decisions.

It is only in the past 15 years, however, that a growing call for a *systematic* sociology of morality has emerged (see, for example, Stivers, 1996; Thiele, 1996; Davydova & Sharrock, 2003; Pharo, 2005; Zdrenka, 2006; Abend, 2008; Ignatow, 2009; Swartz, 2009; Kang & Glassman, 2010). Amongst these, Abend (2008), argues for sociological inquiry into morality focused on 'empirical accounts of people's moral beliefs, and their causes and consequences' (p. 120); Pharo (2005), drawing on Pierre Bourdieu's (1997) social and cultural reproduction theory, argues that the concept of choice, prevalent in conventional moral discourses, be replaced by an analysis of 'social settings [that] do not depend on agents' decisions...[but on] situations like scarcity of goods, lack of political liberty, sexual oppression, restriction of social perspectives' (no page numbers on text); and Thiele (1996) advocates a sociology of morality that investigates the origins and 'disputes' concerning moral authority' (p. 7).

Turning the 'sociological imagination' (Mills, 1959) to a consideration of morality, and answering these questions in a systematic fashion, is especially important when considering morality and moral education in resource-poor contexts. The poor experience poverty not just as economic deprivation but as moral judgement—being poor is often associated with being 'immoral, alcoholic and degenerate...stupid'

(Bourdieu, 1998, p. 43). Sayer (2005) argues that the poor are discriminated against on multiple levels—and such discrimination is a moral issue, worthy of sociological consideration as a *moral*, not merely a *social* phenomenon. In this paper, I propose there are multiple benefits to be derived from pursuing a sociology of morality in general and of moral education in particular. A sociology of morality provides the opportunity to consider lived morality in social context. It invites us to investigate the way in which poverty affects people's moral development and how being morally good reproduces social and economic advantage. A sociology of morality also allows us to evaluate public commentary regarding the moral character of historical and contemporary groups through critical lenses; for example, interrogating calls for 'moral regeneration' (Lu, 2002; Quinlan, 2004) through the lens of 'moral panics' (Cohen, 1980; Ben-Yehuda, 1986). Finally, it challenges the way in which research and practice in the field of moral education has been dominated by philosophical and psychological approaches. In contrast, this theoretical reflection draws upon an empirical study that foregrounds the social and cultural contexts of young people's lived morality in an impoverished environment in South Africa. While I offer some background to this study below, it is reported in detail elsewhere (Swartz, 2007, 2009, see pp. 403–405 for a review) and serves as an example of a social context in which the usual psychological approach to moral development simply cannot apply, due largely to the presence of poverty and the absence of quality education, conditions necessary for linear cognitive development.

Studying the moral lives of poor youth in South Africa

The study upon which this reflection is based explored how young people living in an impoverished South African township understand the concept of morality and how their construction of morality facilitates their processes of moral growth. The term 'township' refers to a black residential area created by the segregationist policies of the former South African government. It is has similarities with a favela in Rio De Janeiro, a slum in Calcutta or Nairobi and a barrio in Colombia or Mexico City. Furthermore, although the levels of poverty are not comparable, in so far as social marginalisation is concerned, it may also be compared with an inner-city urban ghetto in the USA, a banlieue on the outskirts of Paris and a council estate in Glasgow or London. In colloquial terms in South Africa a township is often referred to as *ikasi*.

The study took place in Langa, a periurban township near Cape Town, and follows 37 young men and women aged between 14 and 20, over the course of 16 months. The majority of these youth were in Grade 9 (usually aged 14 to 15) and attended a township school, while a small group commuted to a nearby suburban school. The research design combines the usual elements of ethnography (participant observation, focus groups and interviewing), along with a survey questionnaire and multiple creative methods[1] designed to engage youth over a lengthy period. Overall, the study provides an account of the moral lives of vulnerable young people from within a context of partial-parenting, partial-schooling, pervasive poverty and inequality in the aftermath of the moral injustices of Apartheid. It shows how these young people exhibit conventional values in some areas (substance use, violence, crime), contested values in others (money and sex), as well as postmodern values, especially regarding authority and self-authorisation. The study identifies young people's social representations of morality as action (what you do), as embodied (who you are and who others are to you) and as located or inevitable (where you are, i.e., in school, at home, off the streets or simply in *ikasi*). Despite self-identifying much of their behaviour as 'wrong', young people located themselves as overwhelming 'good', while making it clear that they hold themselves solely responsible for their 'bad' behaviour. In this sociological reflection, I focus on around 80% of these youth, those who comprise two of the four subcultures of township youth, avoiding the two extremes of those who are sheltered and those who are convicted and hardened criminals.[2] While a comprehensive sociology of moral education is beyond the scope of the paper, I offer two conceptual tools towards such a sociology, that of 'moral ecology' and 'moral capital'.

Lived morality—a social or moral ecology

Viewing young people's lived moral context through a sociological lens as a 'moral ecology' can be realised through combining concepts already in common use. The word *ecology* originates from the biological study of the interrelationships between organisms and their environment (such as climate or soil structure). A 'social ecology' (Swanson *et al.*, 2003) is concerned with the web of human relationships within their environmental contexts. Such a perspective readily acknowledges that contexts are complex with human actions affected by the environment, which in turn shapes 'the actions of individuals and communities' (p. 23). Urie Bronfenbrenner's (1979, 1986, 1992) 'ecological systems theory' helps to systematise the study of the environment's effects on people's lives by describing these influences as interconnecting systems. Ironically Bronfenbrenner is a developmental psychologist rather than a sociologist but his framework has appealing sociological application.

The components of a moral ecology

Building on social ecological theory, Bronfenbrenner (1992) defines the *ecology* of human development as:

> the scientific study of the progressive, mutual accommodation, *throughout the life course*, between an active, growing human being, and the changing properties of the immediate settings in which the developing person lives, as this process is affected by the relations between these settings, and by the larger contexts in which the settings are embedded. (p. 188; emphasis in original)

Bronfenbrenner (1992) proposed that human development be considered through a 'hierarchy of systems at four levels moving from the most proximal to the most remote' (p. 226). These four contexts are the *microsystem* (immediate context of work, home and school), the *mesosystem* (interrelationships between microsystems), the *exosystem* (institutions and practices affecting youth) and the *macrosystem* (social and cultural contexts). Later Bronfenbrenner added a fifth context, that of the *chronosystem* (change over time). At the centre of this ecology is the developing young person—with all his or her 'cognitive competence, socio-emotional attributes, and context-relevant belief systems' (p. 228). In keeping with Bronfenbrenner's taxonomy, I have called this the *endosystem*—analogous with the intrapsychic components of human (and moral) development of which we usually speak, to the neglect of socio-cultural contexts.

Outside of the endosystem, the most immediate context for each individual is therefore the microsystem—'a pattern of activities, roles, and interpersonal relations experienced by a developing person in a given face-to-face setting' (Bronfenbrenner, 1992, p. 227). The microsystem in this research study comprises the schools, homes, streets and communities of these township youth. Included in these contexts, in my understanding, are relationships young people have with teachers, peers and other school staff (school); their mothers, fathers, siblings, own offspring and extended and blended families (home); friends, peers, gangs, youth from other parts of the township and romantic or sexual partners (streets); and neighbours, street committees, unrelated older peers, unrelated younger children and religious establishments (community).

At the other extreme Bronfenbrenner (1992) describes various macrosystems, which comprise *'belief systems, resources, hazards, life styles, opportunity structures, life course options, and patterns of social interchange'* (p. 228; emphasis in original). For the young people who participated in the study, the various macrosystems in which they found themselves included: the political contexts of neoliberal fiscal policies; moral regeneration as an official South African discourse; pervasive poverty and its effects on school quality and unequal access to education; and various manifestations of structural injustice peculiar to the South African context, including gender and racial discrimination. Because a macrosystem refers to the prevailing *attitudes* and *ideologies* of a society, a communal culture of violence and corruption, limited practice and experience of human rights and strong ethnic and religious cultural practices are all included in the macrosystem of township youth.

Between micro- and macrosystems lie the mesosystem and the exosystem. The mesosystem describes the interrelationships between microsystems of which young people are a part. For these township youth, the mesosystem consists of interrelationships between home, school, streets and community. In the South African township context, there are few 'linkages' (see Bronfenbrenner, 1979, pp. 210–216) between these systems, especially between home, school and community. Somewhat more contact exists between community and home and tends to be more established than for those of the suburban middle classes, while interactions between communities and streets are often antagonistic. The exosystem also occupies space between micro- and macro-systems and comprises *institutions* and *practices* of which the young person is not directly a part, but whose 'consequences' (p. 227) s/he experiences. In the context of township youth, the criminal justice system, local government policies, adults' general behaviour in society (for example, substance use practices and the prevailing work ethic), parents' workplace conditions, the economy, including health and social services, and mass media all form part of the exosystem.

Finally, Bronfenbrenner (1986) describes the chronosystem as 'changes over time within the person and within the environment' (p. 724) that alter the relationship between the person and the environment. For these township youth, besides obvious changes such as puberty and increasing cognitive sophistication (arguably covered in the endosystem), the chronosystem also includes the move from tribalism, colonialism and Apartheid to living in a nascent democracy. Given South Africa's distinctive history, over time the relations between and within these various systems have changed. For example, young people became less closely monitored and less integrated into kin or culture systems. More substantially, the end of Apartheid removed the object of resistance for many youth and their families who were politically active in the struggle for a democratic state.[3] Figure 1 summarises

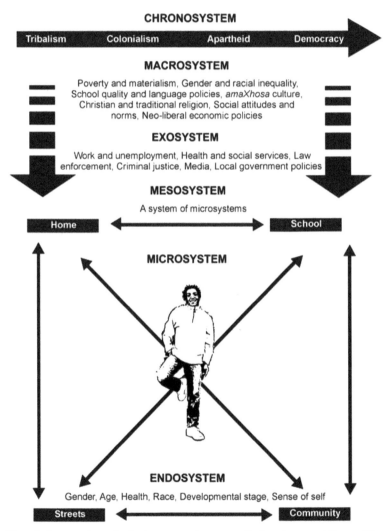

Figure 1.   Bronfenbrenner's ecological systems theory applied to the moral lives of South Africa's township youth

Bronfenbrenner's ecological systems theory as applied to the moral lives of today's township youth.

The relevance of Bronfenbrenner's ecological systems theory of youth development to researching lived morality is to foreground the importance of multiple contexts in youth constructions of morality. It challenges the researcher to consider morality beyond the narrow confines of individual choice or even the close influences of family, peers, school and community. It compels us to expand our vision beyond the psychological focus of cognitive development and to recognise broader socio-cultural forces that interact at multiple levels. The concept offers a meaningful way of talking about moral growth as the sum of its contexts, the influences of different kinds of moral knowledge, constructions of right and wrong and the discordant processes of moral decision making, of an individual and of groups of people. These interactional effects are best understood as complex and interconnecting systems in which combined single effects contribute in unexpected ways to the larger system. Applying the notion of a moral ecological lens to a study of young people's lived experiences and understandings of morality results in the ability to describe, in some depth, the systems at work, including young people's multiple moral positionings, competing influences and complex antinomies and how these change over time.

A moral ecology of interconnecting systems and complex antinomies

In order to show how the notion of a moral ecology may be operationalised, I now turn to a description of the moral lives of the township youth among whom I researched, employing Bronfenbrenner's taxonomy in doing so. Space does not allow me to offer the empirical evidence from which I drew these conclusions (see Swartz 2007, 2009), although I will incorporate some examples by way of illustration.

In the *endosystem*, the youth I studied exhibit a strong sense of self, but are unaware of the socio-emotional deficits they experience as a direct consequence of living in poverty. They strive for agency while at the same time relinquishing agency to 'God', 'witches' and other supernatural forces. They display a clear understanding of right and wrong, while acknowledging a chasm between moral beliefs and moral behaviour. They show deep connections to close kin and friends, but have a limited circle of care that seldom extends beyond these relationships. They seem to respond to epiphanal moments that inspire reform, but their attempts at reform seldom result in long-term change. They articulate willingness for mentoring relationships with adults, but have too few adults positively invested in their lives. They live superficially non-reflective lives, but given the opportunity and adult encouragement are able and willing to do the 'moral work' of reflection.

At the level of *microsystems* young people live in a world created by Apartheid in which survival is difficult and death and violence are everyday occurrences. They have enormous amounts of free-time due to frequent school disruptions and adult caregivers who are either permanently absent or busy making a living by informal means or in poorly paid, long-houred jobs. The result is that youth are socialised on the streets of a community that is at once exciting and caring and violent, retributive and alcohol-sodden. Furthermore, youth, whilst hopeful about their future, seem to be unaware that high unemployment rates and poor education make finding decent work improbable. They profess an enormous desire for education but are disengaged and bored at school and only sporadically attend. They are HIV/AIDS aware and recognise multiple partners as an unacceptable norm, yet succumb to pressure to have multiple sexual partners. Pervasive anger and feelings of loss exist toward 'absent' fathers, while mothers are idealised as moral exemplars (often in the absence of what they consider 'right' behaviour). Young people live in communities that profess collectivism and communalism, but practise harsh retributive justice, selfishness and indifference. They espouse high rates of mobility to escape negative circumstances, yet mobility causes a lack of stability and sheared relationships—both crucial for moral growth. These youth have few recreational and diversionary activities in the township and those they have (e.g. sport and music) are largely untapped as forms of diversion. Television is uncritically consumed in large doses, yet, like sport and music, its educational value remains unexploited. Youth see material acquisitiveness as a means to dignity, yet transgress their own values by stealing in order to acquire drugs, cellphones and clothes. They partake in uncalibrated substance use with little adult sanction and many examples of adult addiction.

At the level of the *macrosystem* young people display a love for beauty despite living in a dirty environment of which they are ashamed. They are not antagonistic to religious faith, but are also not meaningfully engaged in its practices and institutions. They are animated about cultural practices and open to its pedagogic influence, but are waylaid by the excess of alcohol that accompanies many practices. They live in communities that profess an *Ubuntu* ethic of mutual help while at the same time exhibiting community jealousy at individual success. At the level of the *exo*- and *chronosystems* youth see employment as a moral panacea, but harbour unrealistic professional work ideals. They also display an almost crippling sense of personal responsibility and meritocracy, but are unable to articulate the effects of poverty and the causes of current structural injustices.

In the absence of a full account, two stories illustrate how an ecological lens helps to interpret young people's moral lives. Thimna, a tiny 19-year-old young woman, struggled to concentrate at school and showed clear signs of foetal alcohol spectrum disorder (FASD). She constantly dropped out of school due to her inability to focus on her studies. Thimna told me that she had grown up in a '*shebeen* [tavern] house' with her alcoholic mother selling alcohol and that she (Thimna) had begun drinking at 14. Soon she was involved in a gang, and then incarcerated for stealing a cellphone in order to pay for her alcohol. She dropped out of school permanently after falling pregnant and currently struggles to hold down a job as a street sweeper due to her alcoholism. Thimna's moral ecology included physical manifestations of FASD, parental neglect, poor education and substance use—all of which are interrelated.

Luxolo, a stocky, tough, 19 year-old gay woman with a scarred face was trying for the fourth time to pass Grade 9 when I met her. She described her life as 'going wrong' in 1999 when she started drinking, went to high school and met new friends.

She also related how 1999 was the year her father first got in touch with her and then failed to show up for a appointment she had travelled over 1000 miles to keep. Later she ran away from home, 'to escape my mother's boyfriend' and spent a year on the streets of Cape Town. She described how the streets taught her to defend herself, use a knife and disguise her sexual orientation to avoid homophobic violence. Those she met on the street later became her accomplices in armed 'housebreaking'. Her fear of being caught during these robberies led her to drink heavily and take drugs for 'courage'. Her 'drunkenness', in turn, led to 'being beaten up and robbed when I was drunk' and ultimately missing her mother's farewell phone call. (Her mother had repeatedly tried calling her on the weekend she died of an AIDS-related illness.) Finally, Luxolo's experience of ongoing community violence—including a harrowing experience of watching members of her street committee bludgeoning a man suspected of rape to death with a concrete block before tipping a burning brazier over him—led to emotional blunting. She told this and other stories of violence completely dispassionately. When she told me of the time she 'took a knife and stabbed him [her cousin]…over a little thing—he took my food', she was laughing. Perhaps it was inevitable that violence should become normalised through Luxolo's multiple and sustained contact with it. However, what Luxolo's life story does is provide an ecological explanation for her moral behaviour. In spite of this ecology, she still retained a capacity for deep affection, surprising honesty, concern for her reputation and a genuine sense of remorse over her actions.

What is evident, even from these brief stories and the preceding theoretical summary, is a complex portrait of township youth's moral understandings and lives, or moral ecology. It suggests the presence of competing antinomies: on the one hand there are positive facets to the phenomenon being described, while on the other there is a related negative or constraining feature. So, for example, education is lauded and sought after, but teachers are often abusive and young people frequently truant. Of course, not every paradox is present in each young person's life. What is also startlingly clear is that the moral life of young people living in a context of poverty is neither linear and ordered, nor is their moral development directly related to physical maturation, as is often depicted in existing moral development literature focused on youth living in the Global North (Kohlberg *et al.*, 1983; Damon, 1984). In more stable environments moral growth is largely depicted as a series of deliberate choices within a series of narrow options. In the lives of township youth, while options are far wider, the act of choosing is more limited and immediate.

The usefulness of moral ecology in understanding how poverty and morality are linked

Using an ecological lens also showed how young people's moral reasoning ability, the role of personal responsibility for moral (or immoral) action and the context of poverty were interwoven in complex ways. This interplay was crucial to understanding the chasm that exists between young people's stated moral beliefs and their subsequent behaviour. The study found that young people living in poverty lack not so much the *ability* to engage in high order levels of cognitive reflection, but the *opportunity* and resources to do so. If, as various literatures suggest (Yehuda *et al.*, 2001; Evans & English, 2002), poverty results in physical manifestations, such as depression, despair, fatigue (from stress hormone overload), anxiety, apathy, a struggle to delay gratification, emotional blunting, the consequences of FASD and avolition, then it is understandable that youth who live in chronic and pervasive contexts of poverty lack the resources to act on what they know and desire to be right and toward which they aspire. A further example, illustrates this point.

Seventeen year-old Sipho and 19 year-old Vuma, Tapelo and Ingwazi are young men who are members of different street gangs. As is perhaps to be expected, they related accounts of involvement in violence, robbery, hijacking and territorial fighting as a consequence of their gang affiliation. They, too, reflected the normalisation of violence prevalent in *ikasi* when speaking about the pervasive interpersonal violence 'amongst friends' Furthermore, their involvement in petty theft in order to buy drugs and alcohol 'to forget my troubles', as well as designer clothes so they could 'be someone in South Africa', reflects the insidious impact of poverty on human dignity. Frequent runs-ins with the law and near-death experiences resulted in a strong desire to change or reform their lives, but the effect of their environments was often to sabotage these aspirations. These young men wanted to complete school, but failed repeatedly. They wanted to get jobs, but were largely unsuccessful, or only succeeded in getting poorly paid and what they described as 'dirty jobs' (construction work and cleaning). They wanted help to deal with their addictions, but mental health services are not readily available in townships. Consequently, the effects of school drop-out and unemployment resulted in too much free-time to 'do wrong things'; and long-term substance use, especially marijuana, resulted in apathy and physical fatigue—ultimately an inability to act on intentions. These are all sequelae of poverty and prime illustrations of how poverty is complicit in the (im)moral lives of poor youth and why an ecological approach to understanding moral life is essential.

In reflecting on poor youth's lived morality and in answer to the question 'Are poor people more or less moral than their middle-class counterparts?', an ecological lens leads one to conclude that the answer depends largely on what is meant by 'being moral'. If by being moral we mean doing the good, then the answer is yes—some poor youth are less moral than their middle-class counterparts. Poor youth generally report higher levels of risk behaviour than middle-class youth and crime rates are inversely correlated to social class (McCord, 1990). But, if by being moral we mean knowing the good, desiring the good and identifying as a moral self, then the answer is no. The poor youth in this study possessed all three of these facets of morality, but most seemed to lack the resources to act on their beliefs. However, the study showed that meaningful engagement with a caring adult (as I came to be perceived) over the course of a year, being encouraged to reflect on their behaviour and to provide reasons for the 'belief-behaviour' gaps in their lives, their ability (and desire) to reflect grew profoundly. This disconnect between belief and behaviour can therefore be attributed to a resource-poor environment—including poor education (Porteus *et al.*, 2002), a dearth of intermediate associative structures (McLaughlin, 1992) and normative role models (Hertzke, 1998). Of course, young people's resilience plays a large role in overcoming adverse social and economic contexts (Masten, 2001; Buckner *et al.*, 2003) but from a moral growth point of view further sociological tools are necessary for understanding lived morality and providing relevant moral education.

'Moral capital'

The second useful tool for articulating a sociology of moral education is the notion of 'moral capital'. This construct emerged from the field and by interrogating the current literature on social capital. In the field young people regularly spoke of 'being good' as a form of capital. In other words the act of 'being good' resulted in them regularly attending school, completing their education and accessing the job market. Having a job in turn enabled them to 'do good things', like provide for family members. Being good therefore produces economic capital. In addition, these youth identified the necessary elements that would contribute to them becoming good people, which, in sociological terms, may be described as assets or capital. (See, as a counterpoint to this argument, Ramose's explication of *timocracy* in this Special Issue, pp. 291–303). In the next section, I describe the two ways in which the notion of moral capital emerged in the field, compare it to the concept of social capital and draw some conclusions regarding how morality, poverty and social reproduction are related.

How 'being good' is a form of capital

Bourdieu (1997), in his seminal essay 'The forms of capital', describes three types of capital—*economic*, *cultural* and *social*. Economic capital comprises *physical assets* that produce and reproduce profits upon investment. Cultural capital encompasses the forms of knowledge, skill, education or institutionalised advantages a person possesses that provide them with the symbolic means for obtaining and maintaining higher status in society. Social capital comprises the social obligations and networks of trust based on group membership and relationships that serve to confer advantage on individuals and groups. Ultimately, Bourdieu argues that 'every type of capital is reducible in the last analysis to economic capital' (p. 54). His key argument in elucidating the forms of capital was to show how societies are structurally stratified, not dependent on 'simple games of chance...so that everything is not equally possible' (p. 46). In his formulation, the differential possession of cultural and social capital accounts for the reproduction of class through education.

Throughout the study of these Langa youth, young people made the connection between education and achieving future dreams and goals ('If you don't have any education, no future for you') and recognised school as morally empowering, diversionary, a deterrent to crime and the key to future success: 'School is very good, it takes you out of trouble, so if you don't want to be in trouble this keeps you out of trouble' (Ingwazi). Young people repeatedly made the connection between having a job and being a moral person. Poseletso, a 17-year-old young woman, summed up this association most profoundly:

> I think education should be free. Some of them they want to be good people but they don't have money to go to university so that they can study and then become good people when they have got their own jobs. So they don't have money, so they end up staying in the street—doing all those [wrong] things.

'Becom[ing] good people when they have got their own jobs' is a key representation of the relationship between poverty and morality. As these young people spoke of their desire to be good people, and of what being a good person might mean to their immediate and longer-term futures, a dialectical notion of 'morality as capital' suggested itself as an explanatory framework in which morality generates capital and capital generates morality. In other words, being good provides young people with the opportunity to embark on the cycle of 'be a good person, complete school, get a job, be a good person'. In this sense, morality is seen as an instrumental good—it produces economic value. Extrapolating from this data I therefore suggest that moral capital refers to:

> those qualities, capacities, intelligences, strategies, and dispositions that young people acquire, possess, and can 'grow' in the pursuit of moral maturity, and where moral maturity (with its goal of 'being a good person') is related to educational, career, and financial success. Moral capital consists of accruing a record of moral stance, enactment, and reputation. It can be possessed, enlarged, increased, invested in, lost, gained, and transferred. It is recognised by others, creating advantages, and comprises a combination of personal, social, relational, institutional, and structural features that ultimately convey (economic) benefit to those who possess it. (Swartz, 2009, p. 148)

If this definition of moral capital is to be accepted, it raises an important question: How is the possession of moral capital, if at all, connected to the reproduction of social inequalities. In my analysis of poverty and morality (Swartz, 2009), I have shown how young people's moral lives are affected by poverty through the absence of normative regulators, the inability of mediating institutions to be effective pedagogic agents and the physical effects of poverty on mental health functioning crucial to moral decision making. On the evidence of this study, poor youth, whilst not verbalising the effects of poverty and structural injustices on their lives, persist in their efforts (somewhat like trying to swim in oil) to become better people by acknowledging responsibility and aiming to work harder in order to escape their lives of deprivation. As serious as these effects of poverty are on township youth's lived morality there is a further economic effect. Poor youth *depend* on turning moral capital into economic capital. They therefore embrace, rather than resist, 'goodness' or conformity, contrary to existing sociological literature on resistance (Willis, 1981; Giroux, 1983; Hall & Jefferson, 1993; Bourdieu, 1998). In addition, these poor youth recognise the elements that will help them, to become 'good' people. They realise the payback that comes if you are seen by others, especially potential employers or life partners, as a good, honest, hardworking, trustworthy person. Conversely they know what prospects await those who are viewed as serial transgressors—'no future for you'.

What 'capital' is needed to be good?

From the research data, four features of moral capital were identified: (1) relational connection; (2) reflective practice; (3) personal agency; and (4) the importance of an enabling environment. Figure 2 provides a summary of these four main elements of moral capital, with constituent components in each category. Below I describe each in turn and show how they operate as 'capital' in the life of a poor young person.

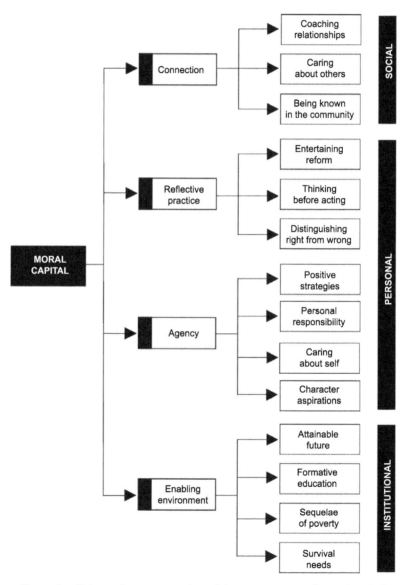

Figure 2. Schematic representation of the components of moral capital

Relational connection. The first element of moral capital relates to the sense of connection young people articulated as a moral influence. They described at length the importance of mothers and younger siblings as exemplary and inspirational moral influences and referred to friends and romantic partners as central to their moral lives. These *caring* relationships provided youth with strong motivations to make sacrificial moral choices, such as voluntarily parting with money earned, and also to work hard at school in order to maximise the possibility of getting a job. Relational connection acted as a resource or form of capital in young people's quest to become good people for the sake of those people who cared about them.

The young people in my study also spoke of how *being known* in their community was a deterrent to doing wrong. Community members who know them will tell parents of bad behaviour. As a result, those who were involved in crime said they limited their activities to places where they were 'not known' so that community members could not 'hunt me down' or 'beat me'. As Sipho told me, 'I only rob the people I don't know—if you know him, you won't rob him'. So, one strategy to help young people acquire greater amounts of relational connection in their communities is to provide opportunities to widen their circle of connection—of those who know them and are known to them.

Perhaps most surprising of all is young people's overt hunger for adult involvement in their lives, people who could 'talk' to them or 'coach' them. Mothers, other family members, older friends and neighbours featured high on the list of those with whom young people wanted to talk. Young people wanted 'coaching relationships' that were long-term, stable and in which they were 'listened to' and 'pushed' but not 'judged' or 'laughed at' (a frequent complaint against teachers). The need to be connected through mentoring seems to be an important part of acquiring moral capital.

Reflective practice. Related to this sense of connection is reflective practice, another feature of moral capital. Frequently, over the course of the study young people told me they tend to be unreflective at the moment of making moral decisions. In Vuma's words, 'If I think before I did something, I will know that that is wrong.' What young people needed was both the opportunity and encouragement to reflect on moral decisions in a systematic way, *prior* to acting, and then guidance to act in keeping with these beliefs. This reflective ability and practice can be considered a form of moral capital because it modulates behaviour that detracts from being a good person.

Over the course of the study and in various activities, young people distinguished clearly between right and wrong and provided reasons for why they judged each to be so. They were also able to reflect on the dissonance between moral belief and moral behaviour. A number spoke of 'knowing the rules', especially surrounding alcohol, violence and crime. Drinking in a friend's shack without girls one might be tempted to 'force into sex'; not carrying a knife when they knew they were going to be drinking; making amends for drunken violence; using a weapon to scare but not harm someone; and not robbing people they know, or women, illustrate some of these rules. While arguably these rules are still appalling, the fact that young people have moral aspirations, take pre-emptive steps to curb the possibility of excessive immoral behaviour, and consider *rules* governing behaviour at all, is evidence of moral capital. It points to the existence of reflection even in the midst of morally wrong behaviour.

Perhaps the richest deposit of moral capital is to be found in young people's intense desire and struggles to *reform* that I observed over the course of the year. Accompanying these desires were often significant moments or 'turning points' (Masten, 2001, p. 233) in their lives. Young people constructed these epiphanies as profound influences on their moral character. For young women, epiphanies included becoming pregnant, the death of a parent or relocating from a rural area to the city. For young men it was a stint in jail, a near-death experience or 'becoming a man' (undergoing a traditional initiation ceremony). For both, the arrival of a new girl- or boyfriend provided the motivation for 'changing my footsteps'. In total I documented 12 complex struggles to reform over 16 months. In fact, a key way in which youth represented themselves as moral people was through repeated reference to reforming and changing. This constant desire for *semper reformanda* ('always reforming' or 'always *about* to be reformed') is a form of moral capital. If young people were happy with their current moral context, reflective practice would be absent.

Personal agency. A third element of moral capital is young people's strong sense of agency. Their struggles to reform, as well as the way in which they displayed responsibility for their behaviour, demonstrate moral agency. The majority told me it was they *alone* who were responsible for bad actions, while others included external factors (such as peer pressure and substance use) but only *in addition* to themselves. Along similar lines, when asked about the kind of person they wanted to be in the future, all but two of the young people's character aspirations were to be good or better people.

A further source of moral capital arose from young people's care for themselves, manifest in concern for their *reputation* in the community. For example, Andiswa, a 15-year-old young woman, told me she decided not to have sex with the men who were buying her drinks in a local tavern because her *reputation* was 'good, and especially amongst the old people', and how smoking marijuana while also regularly attending church was ruining both her and her family's reputation. The existence of young people's care for self (Damon, 1984) is thus a form of moral capital. Damon and Gregory (1997) suggest communities should capitalise on these dispositions to goodness by providing youth with common expectations in the form of a youth charter.

Besides young people's sense of personal responsibility, their character aspirations and their regard for preserving a positive reputation, a few displayed agency in constructing positive strategies to avoid moral harm. Mathsufu deliberately chose making music and engaging in sport to keep him from succumbing to the *ikasi* 'style' of robbery, alcohol and drugs. A number of young people spoke of 'not walking' with wrong friends, even if it meant moving neighbourhoods, changing schools or leaving gangs. These positive strategies are limited, but to the extent that they are present at all are evidence of agency—and agency to 'do right' is a crucial form of moral capital.

That there are limited examples of agency points to the difficulty of sustaining agency, reflective practice and relational connection in the absence of an enabling environment.

Enabling environment. In general, debates about delinquency centre around two opposing poles: 'blame the victim' and 'blame the system' (Giddens & Birdsall, 2001, p. 316). So far, in considering the notion of moral capital, personal and social factors have been taken into consideration. What of systemic, structural, environmental and institutional factors? When I asked research participants to identify factors that might help them to be or become better people, only a few referred to the influence of environmental factors on their lives. For the others, their analysis centred on their own agency in becoming good people. None spoke directly of lacking the resources to act on their good intentions or of the socio-emotional effects of poverty that we now know to impinge on moral decision making. When pushed, however, a number hinted at four enabling factors in the environment that might help them to be better people—and that could therefore be considered a form of moral capital. The strongest was the availability of an *attainable future*, in other words, employment. For most young people, completing schooling and finding a job were the key factors in allowing them to break through the moral glass ceiling imposed by poverty. In the absence of such an attainable future, as youth grow older, they increasingly turn to crime to meet their need for material dignity (Sayer, 2005).

Furthermore, a *formative* education can encourage young people to be reflective and connected and can exemplify democratic processes of living. This would be a form of moral capital. Township schools that are marked by violence, filthy toilets, a lack of recreational space and uncaring, intoxicated and predatory teachers will not achieve these outcomes. Good quality schooling is also likely to contribute to gaining employment. The absence of formative education prevents the acquisition of moral capital.

A third characteristic that thwarts moral capital was the absence of help to cope with the *mental health effects* of living in an environment of poverty. Most alluded to their problems with substance use and Luxolo was amongst only a few who recognised her need to 'commit myself to something else [rather than alcohol and marijuana]'. Few recognised the effects of FASD, the normalisation of violence or the general mental and physical fatigue, depression, apathy, avolition and emotional blunting they experienced as consequences of poverty. Consequently, to deal with these issues as sequelae of poverty requiring mental health intervention, rather than as flaws of character, is to recognise the connection between an enabling environment and moral capital. As Smith and Standish (1997, p. ix) argue:

> [The] insistence on the irreducibility of personal responsibility, not to be shuffled off on the grounds that 'it's all society's fault,' has begun to lead to a denial of the part played by social and political factors: a refusal to accept, for example, that unemployment is causally linked to crime and despair.

Institutional and environmental conditions for the development of moral capital in South African townships are largely absent. Social spending is inadequate given the high levels of unemployment. Young people come to school hungry and leave early, unable to concentrate. Many complain of being unable to study in the noise of cramped shacklands, where late-night work is impossible due to the cost of electricity and the needs of family members who have to sleep early to begin long commutes before sunrise. Too many young people have unmet basic needs and so are unable to fully engage with the cognitive educational content that could aid their moral growth. To ensure that young people develop moral capital they need an enabling environment at school (basic needs and formative education) and an attainable future (employment opportunities and mental health services).

This focus on an enabling environment is not meant to suggest that dealing with poverty will automatically ensure that a society becomes morally good. This is clearly not the case in the Global North, where, despite an enabling environment, many young people remain alienated and disaffected. What I am arguing, however, is that young people need an enabling environment *in addition* to relational connection with friends, family, neighbours and teachers. They need caring adults who will help them to reflect on their beliefs and behaviours and they need to be helped to convert their strong senses of personal agency into moral agency. In the absence of an enabling environment, relational connection, reflective practice and personal agency, these young people will be limited in their endeavours to acquire moral capital and transform such capital into economic advancement and social mobility.

The usefulness of the notion of moral capital in moral education research and practice

If we accept that the lived morality of young people is best considered as an ecological web (or moral ecology) of interconnecting relationships between the personal, social, institutional and environmental, then the notion of moral capital is a valuable analytical tool, with empirical applications. As an analytical concept moral capital urges us to unravel what is usually considered together. In terms of its ability to address issues of *power* and *social exclusion*, moral capital provides a useful counter-point to talk of moral panics and moral deficits. If moral capital is linked both to increased schooling and to relational connection, then poor youth are necessarily disadvantaged. By recording youth discourses of morality and suggesting that the term 'moral capital' be employed by researchers, educators and policymakers we allow the focus to be shifted from what is *absent* in the moral lives of youth, to what is *present*. And that, surely, is of benefit to young people, who are animated by discussion of their own capabilities, instead of indifferent to their much-touted shortcomings.

In the context of South Africa's moral regeneration campaign (see Swartz, 2006), the notion of moral capital has perhaps greater theoretical and practical usefulness than that of 'regeneration'. Besides foregrounding young people's current disposition to moral goodness, it also has the capacity to draw attention to the lack of a morally enabling environment. Furthermore, if moral educators adopted the nurturing of moral capital (personally, socially, and in the environment) as their aim, moral education might be more widely implemented and less contested[4] than it currently is. It would serve to shift the current limited focus away from developing cognitive skills or promoting virtue to include discussions around the implications of a disenabling environment and about strategies for fostering relational connection, developing agency and encouraging reflective practice. If an aim of moral education is to nurture or increase moral capital, then moral behaviour can be analysed with regard to the extent of moral capital already available to an individual or to a group. Youth might be said to be lacking moral capital in *particular* areas, rather than being labelled 'bad', 'delinquent' or 'immoral' overall. This could also result in a more nuanced conversation between the 'blame the victim' and 'blame the system' schools of thought, since *social* and *institutional* factors will become part of the discussion, rather than solely focusing on the *personal* in questions of morality.

Conclusion

This paper has offered two contributions towards a renewed discussion of the sociologies of morality and moral education. First, it has argued that it is productive to study lived human morality as a 'moral ecology'. The overall strength of a notion of moral ecology is to offer an alternative way of seeing and describing the context for moral learning. Considering contexts helps a researcher to see how the usual institutions that might inoculate youth against multiple negative influences exert less influence in resource-poor environments than might be the case in a middle-class context. Such consideration shows how township youth have to choose to opt out of the prevailing *ikasi* culture in favour of moral goodness, unlike their middle-class counterparts, who are protected against harmful moral choices by the presence of normative role models and regulators. This picture of the moral life of township youth, while being morally fraught in many respects, offers insight into how youth construct a moral world in resistance to the prevailing culture. In this study, for example, it became clear that the socio-emotional effects of poverty influence reflective ability and that employment is a moral necessity in the lives of economically impoverished youth. Furthermore, the notion of a moral ecology helps moral educators consider moral life as more complex than only moral action. A definition of what it means to be good must surely include moral knowledge, moral identity and moral desire, in addition to moral action. This has implications for the focus of moral education practice where some elements are stronger than others in young people's lived experience.

Second, the paper has argued that, in contexts of poverty, being a good (or moral) person may be considered a form of capital that is translated into economic and social capital bringing advantage to those who are 'good'. In this sense it offers tentative conclusions regarding the social reproduction of morality and how morality and poverty are related.

Finally, the notions of a moral ecology and moral capital are also closely related to each other as tools in a sociology of moral education. Clearly, the moral ecology of young people in resource-poor communities affects the extent of moral capital they possess and the importance acquiring additional moral capital assumes. In these contexts especially, moral education practice has the ability, like schooling, to entrench equality and justice, rather than reproduce inequalities and injustices.

The purpose of this paper has been to provide a theoretical reflection on what was a substantial empirical project. In so doing, I have not done justice to the many possible implications of approaching moral education research and practice from a sociological perspective. Indeed, many of the applications, at which I only hint, have yet to be worked out. However, to the extent that this paper foregrounds social context and offers sociological tools and provokes discussion and begins a conversation I shall have succeeded in my aim of trying to further understanding of how institutions and economic and social contexts affect human moral functioning.

Acknowledgements

I am enormously indebted to Professor Madeleine Arnot at the University of Cambridge for her inspirational and formative supervision of my doctoral work out of which this paper emanates. The comments of two *JME* reviewers and Dr Monica Taylor are also highly valued.

Notes

1. Included in these methods are the use of photo-voice, 'free lists', 'mind maps' and a 'rank-ordering activity' (explained fully in Swartz, 2009, pp. 175–181). In the digital documentary (or photo-voice) activity young people were asked to photograph the 'good' and 'bad' moral influences in their lives. In 'free lists' youth were invited to compile lists of what they considered to be 'good', 'bad', 'right' and 'wrong'. 'Mind maps' asked for representations of how they perceived themselves to make moral decisions. Finally, the rank ordering invited young people, drawing on their digital documentaries, to rank the moral influences in their lives from strongest to weakest. Each research instrument was used to elicit open-ended data on particular aspects of the research question, such as contexts, constructions, influences and processes, while at the same time overlapping to ensure data triangulation.

2. In Swartz (2009) I describe in detail the four categories of township youth identified by my key informants. 'Mommy's babies' were those who were sheltered and seldom ventured outside their home and families (8% of the sample). Next were 'the right ones'—those who engaged judiciously in township life but whose priority was education and achieving future goals (35%). By far the majority were '*ikasi* boys' and '*ikasi* girls' who comprised 43% of the sample—youth whose substance use was unmodulated and who participated in competitions over sex and fashion, resorting to petty theft in order to achieve the latter. Finally, there were the '*skollies*' (14%) or '*tsotsis*'—young people who had already become criminals, drug dealers and committed gangsters. I estimate that these proportions were similarly reflected in the general township youth population.

3. Two reviewers have pointed out the need to expand on my analysis of the chronosystem by referring to how the moral lives of township youth differed under Apartheid and post-Apartheid. This is a salient suggestion that deserves separate attention. I begin the analysis in Swartz (2009, pp. 17–28).

4. Frequently moral education is not implemented in schools because those responsible are unsure about whose values ought to be taught. In the approach I suggest this becomes a non-issue, and moral education becomes Socratic in nature, with all values being questioned and young people being asked to reflect on how they believe they ought to live.

References

Abell, P. (1991) *Rational choice theory* (Brookfield, VT, E. Elgar).

Abend, G. (2008) Two main problems in the sociology of morality, *Theory & Society*, 37(2), 87–125.

Anderson, E. (1999) *Code of the street: decency, violence and the moral life of the inner city* (London, Norton).

Bauman, Z. (1993) *Postmodern ethics* (Oxford, Blackwell).

Baumgartner, M. P. (1988) *The moral order of a suburb* (New York, Oxford University Press).

Bellah, R. (1996) *Habits of the heart: individualism and commitment in American life* (London, University of California Press).

Ben-Yehuda, N. (1986) The sociology of moral panics: toward a new synthesis, *Sociological Quarterly*, 27(4), 495–513.

Bourdieu, P. (1997) The forms of capital, in: A. Halsey, H. Lauder, P. Brown & A. Stuart Wells (Eds) *Education: culture, economy and society* (Oxford, Oxford University Press).

Bourdieu, P. (1998) *Acts of resistance: against the new myths of our time* (Cambridge, Polity).

Bourdieu, P., Chamboredon, J. C., Passeron, J. C. & Krais, B. (1991) *The craft of sociology: epistemological preliminaries* (New York, Walter de Gruyter).

Bronfenbrenner, U. (1979) *The ecology of human development: experiments by nature and design* (Cambridge, MA, Harvard University Press).

Bronfenbrenner, U. (1986) Ecology of the family as a context for human development: research perspectives, *Developmental Psychology*, 22(6), 723–742.

Bronfenbrenner, U. (1992) Ecological systems theory, in: R. Vasta (Ed.) *Six theories of child development* (London, Jessica Kingsley).

Buckner, J.C., Mezzacappa, E. & Beardslee, W.R. (2003) Characteristics of resilient youths living in poverty: the role of self-regulatory processes, *Development and Psychopathology*, 15(1), 139–162.

Cohen, S. (1980) *Folk devils and moral panics: the creation of the Mods and Rockers* (Oxford, M. Robertson).

Damon, W. (1984) Self understanding and moral development from childhood to adolescence, in: W. M. Kurtines & J. L. Gewirtz (Eds) *Morality, moral behavior and moral development* (New York, Wiley).

Damon, W. & Gregory, A. (1997) The youth charter: towards the formation of adolescent moral identity, *Journal of Moral Education*, 26(2), 117–130.

Davydova, I. & Sharrock, W. (2003) The rise and fall of the fact/value distinction, *Sociological Review*, 51(3), 357–375.

Durkheim, E. (1973a) *Moral education: a study in the theory and application of the sociology of education* (E. Wilson & H. Schnurer, Trans.) (New York, Free Press).

Durkheim, E. (1973b) *On morality and society: selected writings* (Chicago, University of Chicago Press).

Evans, G. W. & English, K. (2002) The environment of poverty: multiple stressor exposure, psycho-physiological stress and socioemotional adjustment, *Child Development*, 73(4), 1238–1248.

Fein, M.L. (1997) *Hardball without an umpire: the sociology of morality* (Westport, CN, Praeger).

Foucault, M. (2000) *Ethics: subjectivity and truth* (P. Rabinow, Ed.) (London, Penguin Books).

Giddens, A. & Birdsall, K. (2001) *Sociology* (Cambridge, Polity).

Giroux, H. A. (1983) Theories of reproduction and resistance in the new sociology of education: a critical analysis, *Harvard Educational Review*, 53(3), 257–293.

Granovetter, M. S. & Swedberg, R. (2001) *The sociology of economic life* (Boulder, CO, Westview Press).

Habermas, J. (1990) *Moral consciousness and communicative action* (Cambridge, MA, MIT Press).

Hall, S. & Jefferson, T. (1993) *Resistance through rituals: youth subcultures in post-war Britain* (London, Routledge).

Hertzke, A. D. (1998) The theory of moral ecology, *Review of Politics*, 60(4), 629–659.

Ignatow, G. (2009) Why the sociology of morality needs Bourdieu's habitus, *Sociological Inquiry*, 79(1), 98–114.

Kang, M. J. & Glassman, M. (2010) Moral action as social capital, moral thought as cultural capital, *Journal of Moral Education*, 39(1), 21–36.

Kohlberg, L., Levine, C. & Hewer, A. (1983) *Moral stages: a current formulation and a response to critics* (New York, Karger).

Lauder, H. (2006) *Education, globalization, and social change* (Oxford, Oxford University Press).

Levinas, E. (1987) *Collected philosophical papers* (A. Lingis, Trans.) (Dordrecht, The Netherlands, Kluwer Academic).

Lu, C. (2002) Justice and moral regeneration: lessons from the Treaty of Versailles, *International Studies Review*, 4(3), 3–25.

Luckmann, T. (1983) *Life-world and social realities* (London, Heinemann Educational Books).

Marx, K. (1988) *The Communist manifesto* (F. Bender, Ed.) (London, Norton).

Masten, A. S. (2001) Ordinary magic, *American Psychologist*, 56(3), 227–238.

McCord, J. (1990) Problem behaviors, in: S. S. Feldman & G. R. Elliott (Eds) *At the threshold: the developing adolescent* (Cambridge, MA, Harvard University Press).

McLaughlin, T. H. (1992) Citizenship, diversity and education: a philosophical perspective, *Journal of Moral Education*, 21(3), 235–250.

Mills, C. W. (1959) *The sociological imagination* (New York, Oxford University Press).

Parsons, T. (1937) *The structure of social action: a study in social theory with special reference to a group of recent European writers* (New York, McGraw-Hill).

Pharo, P. (2005) Moral sociology and practical responsibility. Paper presented at the *Max-Planck Institut für ethnologische Forschung Rethinking Moralities Workshop*, La Halle, France, 15–16 December.

Porteus, K., Motala, S., Ruth, T., Tleane, C., Tshoane, M. & Vally, S. (2002) *Values, education and democracy: opening pathways for dialogue* (Pretoria, Wits Education Policy Unit Consortium).

Quinlan, S. (2004) Physical and moral regeneration after the terror: medical culture, sensibility and family politics in France, 1794–1804, *Social History*, 29(2), 139–164.

Sayer, R. A. (2005) *The moral significance of class* (Cambridge, Cambridge University Press).

Simmel, G. (1950) *The sociology of Georg Simmel* (K. Wolff, Trans.) (Glencoe, IL, Free Press).

Smith, R. & Standish, P. (1997) *Teaching right and wrong: moral education in the balance* (Stoke-on-Trent, Trentham).

Stivers, R. (1996) Towards a sociology of morality, *International Journal of Sociology and Social Policy*, 16(1–2), 1–14.

Suttles, G. D. (1968) *The social order of the slum: ethnicity and territory in the inner city* (Chicago, University of Chicago Press).

Swanson, D. P., Spencer, M. B., Harpalani, V., Dupree, D., Noll, E., Ginzburg, S. & Seaton, G. (2003) Psychosocial development and ethnically diverse youth: conceptual and methodological challenges in the twenty-first century, *Development and Psychopathology*, 15(3), 743–771.

Swartz, S. (2006) A long walk to citizenship: morality, justice and faith in the aftermath of apartheid, *Journal of Moral Education*, 35(4), 551–570.

Swartz, S. (2007) The moral ecology of South Africa's township youth. Unpublished PhD thesis, University of Cambridge, UK.

Swartz, S. (2009) *The moral ecology of South Africa's township youth* (New York, Palgrave Macmillan).

Thiele, S. (1996) *Morality in classical European sociology: the denial of social plurality* (Lewiston, NY, E. Mellen Press).

Weber, M. (1978) *Economy and society: an outline of interpretative sociology* (G. Roth & C. Wittich, Eds) (Los Angeles, University of California Press).

Weber, M. (2002) *The Protestant ethic and the spirit of capitalism* (Los Angeles, Roxbury).

Willis, P. E. (1981) *Learning to labor: how working class kids get working class jobs* (New York, Columbia University Press).

Wilson, E. O. (1975) *Sociobiology: the new synthesis* (Cambridge, MA, Belknap Press).

Yehuda, R., Halligan, S. L. & Grossman, R. (2001) Childhood trauma and risk for PTSD: relationship to intergenerational effects of trauma, parental and cortisol excretion, *Development and Psychopathology*, 13(3), 733–753.

Zdrenka, M. T. (2006) Maria Ossowska, *Journal of Classical Sociology*, 6(3), 311–331.

Continuity and change in the development of moral education in Botswana

Yonah H. Matemba

University of Glasgow, Scotland, UK

This article traces the development of moral education (ME) in Botswana from pre-colonial times to the present day. It shows how during this time ME has undergone three distinct phases of development, each emphasising a particular ideology. In pre-colonial times ME was offered as part of indigenous education in the home and community, both formally and informally, directly and indirectly. During the missionary/colonial period (1870s–1966) and in the first three decades of Botswana's independence (1967–1998), ME was taught in the formal school curriculum as an aspect of religious education. During this period religious education was confessional, using Christian moral values as a yardstick in exploring the material content of the syllabus. Since the national educational reforms of the 1990s, ME has undergone a paradigm shift, whereby it has become disengaged from religious education and secularised as a stand-alone subject in the junior secondary curriculum. This paper examines each of these three phases of development, and concludes by offering an assessment of the efficacy of the current phase, given the religiosity of Botswana as a country and the consequences of previous teacher training with ME having been located within religious education.

Introduction and background

This paper analyses three distinct phases of continuity and change in the development of moral education (ME) in Botswana from pre-colonial times to the current day and offers a critique of the current ideology with regard to ME, both as a *secularised* and *stand-alone* subject within the school curriculum. Nigeria excepted (Iheoma, 1985), what makes Botswana unique and worthy of consideration is that it is perhaps the only country in sub-Saharan Africa to have successfully introduced ME as a secular and independent subject into the national curriculum. In many countries in Africa, ME is offered as a subset of other curricular areas, such as spiritual and moral education in Zambia (Simuchimba, 2001), religious and moral education (RME) in Malawi (Matemba, 2009) and life orientation in South Africa (Van

Deventer, 2009). A paper documenting the various phases—cultural, religious and as a stand-alone secular subject—in the development of ME in Botswana is therefore useful in highlighting various lessons for other parts of the African continent either contemplating, or in the process of, revising their approach to ME.

In order to situate the discussion in its appropriate context, some background information about Botswana should be noted. In general, Botswana provides an exception to the stereotypes of corruption and autocracy found in parts of sub-Saharan Africa. It has the longest running democratic system of government anywhere on the continent. It is also *not* an impoverished country, unlike many others in sub-Saharan Africa. Despite being landlocked, economically the country is a star performer with impressive foreign reserves of more than US$9 billion (Kumo, 2009). Considered the least corrupt country in Africa, Botswana is also attractive to international investors (Mafirakurewa, 2009). Such economic success has come about in part due to its small population (just under two million people), political stability, free-market economic policies and fiscal prudence in the management of diamond export earnings (Conteh, 2008).

With regard to religious affiliation, Botswana has a predominantly Christian population (83%), with 11% recording no religious affiliation. African traditional religion is the largest religious minority (4%), while adherents to other religions (i.e. Islam, Hinduism, the Baha'i Faith and Sikhism) make up 2% of the population (Haron & Jensen, 2008). Ethnically, the country is also diverse, comprising eight 'major' Tswana groups,[1] who make up 79% of the population, and a number of so-called 'minor'[2] tribes. Despite this diversity, the country remains one of the most peaceful in Africa (Adeyemi, 2007).

Despite the country's positive economic and democratic advances, it has its own share of social ills, not only among youth but in the wider population as well. In recent decades there has been a worrying trend of so called 'passion killings'—young men killing their girlfriends/wives in a fit of jealousy and then themselves committing suicide (Tsayang et al., 2006). Botswana also has an escalating incidence of HIV infection, along with high levels of multiple partnerships, unprotected and hence reckless sexual relationships, exacerbated by escalating incidents of gender-based violence (Renwick, 2007).

Indigenous education as moral education

Moral education in pre-colonial Botswana (i.e. prior to 1870) was rooted in an indigenous system of education which taught young people cultural and moral values. The main aim of this traditional education was to inculcate the *Botho* (or *Ubuntu*) moral code that highlighted virtues such as the importance of community and observance of communal and cultural practices (Gaie & Mmolai, 2007). As was the case throughout Africa, indigenous education in pre-colonial Botswana was provided through both formal and informal methods. Informal education was based on indirect ways of teaching and learning. As children played, engaged in societal practices (such as worship, funerals, marriage and hunting) and interacted with parents, relatives and other adults they became knowledgeable, not only about the essentials of their culture, but also about the expected personal and social moral values of the community. Other informal means of inculcating moral values included songs, dances, proverbs, riddles and stories to teach children to be on their guard against recklessness, evil and trickery. The indirect methods allowed children to observe, learn and internalise unspoken assumptions and prevailing moral values in their homes and the neighbourhood, and the unpleasant consequences that might follow for any infraction of the moral code (Mgadla, 1989).

On the other hand, formal indigenous education in pre-colonial Botswana came mainly through initiation schools known as *bogwera* (for boys) and *bojale* (for girls). Initiation practices in Botswana included a standardised curriculum, a formal means of assessment, set times for instruction and institutional arrangements to promote moral growth along the development continuum. At these initiation schools young people were taught all aspects of traditional life—survival skills, customs, values, marriage, parenting, religion and respect for others—in a formal setting under the tutelage of experienced, specifically appointed village instructors.

Schapera (1978), Mautle (2001), Amanze (2002) and others have provided important details regarding the structure and process of initiation practices in Botswana. *Bogwera*, which lasted four years, was attended by boys between the ages of 12 and 17 years and comprised two stages. The first stage known as *bogwane* began when boys turned 12 years. Instruction occurred in the village, with children sometimes being taken away to a secluded area for parts of this period.

The *bogwane* curriculum consisted of instruction in societal norms, sex education, traditional taboos, agricultural activities and self-defence. Obedience was taught through informing the boys of the consequences of disobedience. Those who were disobedient were told they would 'feel the wrath of the vultures' (Mautle, 2001, p. 27) when they entered *bogwera* proper—the second stage of initiation. During *bogwane*, besides being warned of the consequences of bad behaviour, boys were also told about rewards for obedience and good behaviour, for example that there would be public praise for those acquitting themselves well. Taboos relating to sex were also taught. Instructors pointed out the hazards of indulging in sexual intercourse before penile circumcision and the consequences of breaching taboos (Brown, 1921). These consequences included the shame of early pregnancy and the cultural stigma of being labelled 'promiscuous'. Clearly such taboos were meant to discourage boys from indulging in sexual intercourse until they were mature enough to understand its consequences. As they neared graduation the neophytes underwent an internship phase in which they had to practise the skills learnt and display the behaviours acquired in the presence of relatives who had themselves completed initiation.

After the long preparatory stage of *bogwane*, boys (now young men) were accepted for *bogwera*, during which stage the new initiates were circumcised. The *bogwera* curriculum included showing honour and obedience to the chief and elderly and abstaining from excessive drinking. Topics concerning sex and married life, along with the taboos associated with these, took centre stage during *bogwera*. Instruction included the physiology of sexual relations, procreation, how to conduct themselves in marriage and the 'dangers' of sexual relations with ritually unclean women such as *batsetsi* (new mothers) and widows.

When girls reached puberty they entered the initiation process known as *bojale* which lasted only three months. During *bojale* young women wore thorny attire and painted their faces with fine clay (*letsoku*). As part of *bojale*, clitoridectomy was performed on the girls. The curriculum of *bojale* included topics such as motherhood, respect for elders and husbands, general behaviour towards men, female hygiene and handling household chores (Mgadla, 1989). In addition, child-bearing appears to have been a topic of emphasis. Mautle (2001) reports that one ritual required initiates to walk with their heads bowed and arms folded over their breasts. Then they would sit in a squatting position while being forbidden from looking around 'because the foetus would never do that' (p. 31).

The shortcomings of these traditional forms of ME for both young men and women in pre-colonial times are clearly apparent. On the whole, initiation schools were not for the fainthearted. Run with military-like discipline, initiates were awoken at the crack of dawn, sometimes with a splash of cold water over their bodies. Flogging was common for those that were reported to have been disrespectful to parents and elders before entering *bojale* or *bogwera*. Death in the initiation camps was not uncommon. The most common cause of death seems to have been related to the unsanitary procedures involving penile circumcision for boys and clitoridectomy for girls. When this happened the dead were buried on the same day inside the camp close to the group's fireplace. Such deaths were closely-guarded secrets in the camps and outsiders, including the family of the deceased, were not told while the initiation ceremony was in progress. Indigenous ME in Botswana through initiation practices might be criticised for its inherent authoritarianism and for placing too much emphasis on the needs and interests of the community at the expense of the rights of the individual. Clearly, young people were given little choice in deciding on the values they favoured or wanted to follow.

The account above highlights the important role played by informal cultural instruction—as well as the formal initiation practices of *bojale* and *bogwera*—in how children received moral instruction in traditional society in Botswana. It has been emphasised that until they had passed through *bogwera* or *bojale* a young person in Botswana was considered a 'child', with the implication that, regardless of age, they could not be accorded respect or be allowed to marry. For a man it meant that one could not speak at the *kgotla* (traditional assembly) or even 'inherit his father's estate' (Denbow & Phenyo, 2006, p. 22). Indigenous education in Botswana thus played a crucial role in providing a structured way of inculcating moral values in the young and in particular, provided instruction on matters of self-restraint, morality, respect and obedience, which not only galvanised society towards a common purpose, but also gave youth clear instruction for the future. However, when Western education was introduced during the second half of the nineteenth century, African moral values, and the institutions and practices that shaped them, were largely condemned by missionaries and colonialists as being obstacles to a more desirable system of thought, practice and religion.

Religious education as an agent for moral education

'Christianisation' of moral education

Christianity arrived in Botswana in the mid-1870s and within a short period of time had taken root in the country. Unlike in other African countries, Christianity in Botswana quickly achieved success, for two reasons. First, people converted *en masse* to Christianity following the *dikgosi* (chiefs) and their families, who were the first to be converted. In traditional society commoners were unquestioningly loyal to their *dikgosi* and many simply joined the 'new' religion of their leaders (Mgadla, 1989). The second and related reason is that in Botswana many *dikgosi* actually invited missionaries to set up bases in their chiefdoms. At a time when the country was becoming attractive to white settlers, prospectors, hunters, traders and the well-armed and restless Afrikaner trekkers (from the South), *dikgosi* strategically sought the friendship of missionaries who they believed could source guns and provide advice on how to deal with the influx of other, less desirable, white foreigners in their territories (Ramsay *et al.*, 1996).

One of the main tasks of missionary work in Botswana was the establishment of schools. At the centre of the curriculum offered in the mission schools was the Bible. This was used both as a textbook for religious education (RE) and, more generally, as a reference for teaching Christian moral values. In this context, both missionaries and colonial administrators considered the practice of *bogwera* and *bojale* as obstacles in the expansion and consolidation of the Christian faith. Consequently, Batswana (people of Botswana) and their *dikgosi* were urged to eradicate these institutions in favour of Christianity. Western education provided by missionaries thus replaced indigenous education as the vehicle through which ME was taught. In turn, in the mission schools that flourished, RE became the new vehicle through which ME was now offered; in fact, the purpose of RE in the mission schools was to transmit normative Christian moral values (Ramsay *et al.*, 1996).

While in general it seemed that tribal groups had accepted Christianity as a new way of life, there were those who wanted aspects of traditional culture to continue to guide the moral development of their children, insisting that *bogwera/bojale* had a positive role to play in the moral development of young people. Privately, colonial officials and missionaries began to admit that *bogwera/bojale* had a good effect on discipline, sexual restraint, obedience and in moderating excessive drinking. However, the use of *bongaka* (traditional medicine) and the practice of circumcision made it impossible for missionaries and colonialists to accept a return of *bogwera/bojale* practices (Amanze, 2002).

Educational reforms and the continued poverty of moral education

In spite of the fact that colonial rule in Botswana ended in 1966, the country continued to use the Christian colonial curriculum in schools until the mid-1970s. In 1975 the government set up the First National Commission on Education (FNCE) whose mandate was to review the country's educational system. In 1977 the

Commission produced its report (Botswana Government, 1977), whose recommendations charted the way for the country's new educational system in keeping with the self-governing aspirations of an independent African nation. Underlying the new educational policy was *kagisanyo* (social harmony), a Tswana cultural philosophy that promotes virtuous behaviour and conduct for the common good. *Kagisanyo* is based on the African humanist philosophy of *Botho* and was introduced in education to galvanise young people to national ideals, such as unity, social justice, interdependence and mutual assistance (Marope, 1996).

Among other things, the new educational policy was an attempt to redirect education so that it could focus on values that fostered cultural identity, self-esteem and citizenship. In particular, it aimed to develop in children 'a sound moral code of behaviour compatible with the ethics and traditions of Botswana' (Botswana Government, 1977, p. 5). However, in spite of policy changes on issues such as access to education through the building of new schools, increased capacity in teacher training and restructuring of the education system, the FNCE contained very little in terms of subject reform. For this reason, syllabus content largely remained as it had been prior to the 1977 policy. For instance, ME continued to be offered as a sub-unit of RE with its ideology tied to Christian moral values, as had been the case before independence (Pandey & Moorad, 2003).

Furthermore, the post-independent era in Botswana brought its share of youth problems, such as theft, anti-social behaviour and substance abuse (Balogi, 2004). In this connection, people were particularly critical of RE (and its ME component) for failing to address the moral problems faced by young people (Awino *et al.*, 2004). In fact, as a public response to what was generally perceived as 'moral degeneration' among youth, *bogwera* was revived in the Kgatleng district in 1975 and continued until 1989 (Makgala, 2009). Events in Kgatleng district, which engendered heated radio debates during 1975 and 1976, centred on how society could deal with young people's perceived deteriorating moral standards. Concerned listeners expressed the view that perhaps the solution to the moral malaise lay in the re-introduction of *bogwera*—the old and well-tried methods of the initiation school (Schapera, 1978). In some sense the public attachment to *bogwera* exhibited in the radio debates affirmed Africa's lasting affinity with its tradition and culture which, although on the surface appears to have been seriously undermined by Christian and Western influences, remains intact in the 'sub-conscious depths of [the] African psyche' (Mbiti, 1991, p. 265).

The inability of RE to address the moral issues of young people seems to have also been a concern of other African educators. By the early-1970s a number of countries in the region had begun discussing how RE could be made more responsive to the needs of youth. Between 1970 and 1972 an inter-denominational committee of Protestant and Catholic churches—comprising delegates from several countries in east and central Africa—met and agreed to reform RE so that the subject could respond to the moral challenges faced by African children in a post-independence setting. Following these meetings, a new syllabus for schools, which adopted a life-themes approach, was developed (Pastoral Institute of Eastern Africa, 1974).

In Botswana the east-central African RE syllabi were adopted for both junior and senior secondary schools in 1979/1980 (Awino *et al.*, 2004). To some degree the new programme was a breath of fresh air for RE because it explored contemporary moral issues affecting African youth, such as sex, marriage, justice and service to society. However, the ME components in the east-central African syllabi were still being offered through the lens of Christianity. As before, the primary aim of these materials remained to inculcate Christian moral values (Lindfield, 1986) rather than offer young people the opportunity to choose between alternatives. In addition, these syllabi excluded African indigenous issues and content. In fact it is worth pointing out that while the new material acknowledged the strong undercurrent of traditional religiosity in an African setting, it concluded that traditional religion was a hindrance to Christian work in Africa (Pastoral Institute of Eastern Africa, 1974). This meant that the approach to ME through a revised RE syllabus still failed to produce a curriculum relevant to the socio-cultural context of the contemporary African child in Botswana.

Towards a secular pedagogy for moral education

Almost two decades after the implementation of the recommendations of FNCE, the government instituted a further review of the educational system. In 1993 the Second National Commission on Education (SNCE) was constituted and this once again changed the ideology of ME, along with the medium through which it was taught (Botswana Government, 1993). During the consultation process[3] SNCE noted the paradigm shifts in ME discourses, particularly the impact that moral development approaches and secular pedagogies in values education were having on the subject. For example, Lawrence Kohlberg (1969) and others, such as Paul Hirst (1974), argued that there is a logical distinction between religion and morality, pointing out that while moral development can be premised on faith, it is equally possible (even desirable) to conduct ME independent of religion. In the words of Kohlberg (1974):

> While moral development has a larger context including faith, it is possible to have a public moral education which has a foundation independent of religion. We believe that the public school should engage in moral education and that the moral basis of such education centres on universal principles of justice, not broader religious and personal values. (p. 5)

Others, of course, continue to point out that belief and moral commitment are inescapably tied together in one ultimate vision and, as such, religion should be the epistemological basis for judging moral behaviour (Greer, 1983).

Returning to the consultation process in Botswana, the SNCE observed that some countries had already put into practice some of the scholarly ideas that were emerging in the field of ME, in particular regarding the religious–ME separation. It noted, for example, that Nigeria had an independent and secular ME syllabus as part of its national curriculum (Iheoma, 1985). Also, by this time, countries such as Canada (Canada Government, 1991) and the USA (Purpel, 1998) were teaching a secularised version of ME called 'values education'. The SNCE also became aware of the

British experience (Matemba, 2005), particularly developments in Scotland where in the early 1990s ME and RE in non-denominational state schools had been fused together and taught as RME (McKinney & Conroy, 2007).

At the end of the consultation process the SNCE produced a preliminary report, which made several recommendations on the future direction of Botswana's school curriculum. Regarding RE and ME, the report suggested that the two subjects be fused into a new subject called RME (Botswana Government, 1993). While the ideological approach of the new RME syllabus would remain Christian by explicitly emphasising Christian moral issues, the government was attempting to place moral values and education high on the educational agenda. This, it would seem, was done to address some of the criticisms that had been levelled against the previous syllabus, of ME through RE. The preliminary SNCE report was then sent to stakeholders for comment. A revised version of the report, taking into account critical comments received, was published in 1994 under the title *Revised National Policy on Education* (RNPE) (Botswana Government, 1994). In the RNPE the proposed RME programme was abandoned. Instead, RNPE recommended that ME should be separated from RE. The rationale for this separation was that although the education system had always recognised the importance of ME in the moral development of children, it had never given the subject the attention it deserved. Later, when describing the ME syllabus, the government went further, noting that:

> For a long time, it has been perceived that morality arises from religion and draws its sanction from the same. In our contemporary pluralistic Botswana society, it becomes difficult to talk about a particular set of morals based on one faith since religious affiliation is diverse. It is henceforth imperative to talk of morality that is all encompassing, that is, one that emanates from religion *and* other philosophies of life. Though it has been taught in conjunction with religious education, the two are *not* the same. Therefore there is need to separate moral education from religious education. (Botswana Government, 1998, p. I, emphasis added)

Another significant development for ME in the RNPE was its inclusion in the list of *core* subjects within the junior secondary curriculum. The rationale given for elevating the status of ME was because of its importance in developing shared values among children from diverse religious backgrounds. Religious education remained an optional subject to cater for those wishing to study religion, as provided for in the Education Act (Botswana Government, 1994).

In 1997 the government instituted an *ad hoc* taskforce to design a ME course and the following year a new ME programme was introduced for junior secondary students. It should, however, be noted that the new ME programme was introduced two years after other curriculum subjects had been implemented. The reasons for this late introduction are important to understand. First, the delay was caused by structural, syllabus and staffing issues that had not been worked out in time. In Botswana, each curriculum subject has senior education officers in four crucial areas: (1) curriculum development and evaluation; (2) examinations, research and testing; (3) administration at the Ministry of Education headquarters; and (4) regional education offices. When it came to ME, no education officer had been appointed to any of these areas since none was appropriately qualified. This also meant that the development of the teaching syllabus itself was delayed due to a lack of experts because none in the ME *ad hoc* taskforce had any experience in the subject (Botswana Government, 1998). However, once the syllabus was drawn up, a senior education officer, responsible for RE in the department of secondary education, was given the added responsibility of overseeing the introduction of the ME programme. Then, in 2001, an education officer, responsible for ME in the department of curriculum and development, was appointed and the following year the officer was sent to study in Australia for a master's degree in ME.

Secondly, even when a syllabus was available, schools could not introduce the subject since the country had no trained ME teachers. Teacher training in ME at the national colleges of education for secondary school teachers only commenced in 1998, with the effect that the first cadre of teachers entered the classroom in 2001, three years after the subject was introduced at school level. The University of Botswana—the country's sole public university—enrolled its first group of trainees in ME in the 2002/2003 academic year for a four-year course. Thus the first cohort of ME teachers only graduated in 2006. In spite of this lack of trained ME teachers, the government instructed schools to introduce the subject to be taught by RE teachers, whose teaching loads were reduced to accommodate their new responsibility. In turn, untrained teachers with only 'O'-level education were recruited to teach some of the RE classes. In addition, foreign teachers from Britain, Guyana and India were also recruited to help launch the new ME syllabus. To assist RE teachers in their new roles as ME teachers a series of in-service workshops were held throughout the country where, in particular, the secular ideology and neutral pedagogy was explained.

Another challenge ME faced was the absence of teaching materials, particularly textbooks. Books written specifically for the syllabus appeared towards the end of 1999. This meant that for a whole year in 1998 and the first two school terms (January–August) of 1999, schools had no ME textbooks. It is worth pointing out that some of these books were badly printed, had scant information and were poorly presented (Scanlon, 2000). In some cases, content was offensive to teachers and students alike. For example, in an effort to contextualise materials, one book used a hyena to depict all that is evil (vices) and an impala for all that is good (virtues) (Clarke, 1999). By depicting a hyena in such negative terms, the book could inadvertently be seen to confirm negative cultural perceptions held by Africans associating the hyena with witchcraft and the supernatural. These stereotypes, in turn, exacerbate unhelpful attitudes towards wildlife conservation. The irony of depicting animals in such negative terms is that the tourist industry, which currently accounts for 16% of GDP (Botswana Press Association, 2008), relies on safari excursions where wild animals, including hyena, are a huge attraction (Zeppel, 2007).

Recent developments in moral education

In 2007 the government undertook a general review of junior secondary school syllabi. As such both RE and ME syllabi have been revised with the view to rectify some of the anomalies inherent in the original syllabi of the two subjects (see Matemba, 2005). For example, the revised programme has addressed the duplication of topics that were in the first RE and ME syllabi on issues such as abortion, murder, suicide, euthanasia, human rights and family life, which were included in both syllabi. In the revised syllabi, these topics have been reassigned to ME while RE has been given new topics dealing with typically religious issues. As noted above, there are critics of this reassignment. Other contentious issues in the revised ME syllabus have been removed. For example, a former teaching objective required learners to 'debate a moral dilemma related to a social institution such as birth control in the Roman Catholic Church and wife burning in Hinduism' (Botswana Government, 1996, p. 7). Also significant is that the topic dealing with HIV/AIDS has been retained in both the ME and RE syllabi, perhaps to emphasise the gravity of the pandemic and government's serious intent in addressing it.

The implementation of the revised ME syllabus commenced in schools in January 2010 and comprises four modules spread over three years, as follows:

(1) *Morality*: morality and values, decision-making, moral dilemmas;
(2) *Personal moral issues*: self-concept, inter-personal relationships, adolescence, family life, agents of change in the community, abstinence, sex education, teenage pregnancy, contraception, death and bereavement, abortion, suicide, euthanasia;
(3) *Social moral issues*: HIV and AIDS and sexually transmitted infections, infertility, social justice, citizenship, traditions and the law, crime, punishment;
(4) *Global moral issues*: the concept of human rights, children's rights, child care, rights and roles of animals, bioethics, work ethics, environmental ethics (Botswana Government, 2007a).

Some comments on the content of the syllabus should be made. It is evident that much of its material is underscored by *Botho*. This is exemplified by topics dealing with the values of compassion and respect, the importance of family, indispensability of community and imperatives of social justice. Cultural issues under the topic 'traditions' have also been given some prominence as an acknowledgement of the multicultural (and ethnic) nature of modern Botswana. In keeping with its nationalistic goals, citizenship also features in the syllabus. Furthermore, in an attempt to address contemporary youth moral issues, the syllabus addresses crimes related to sexual relationships—commonly known as 'passion killings', as described at the outset of the paper. This topic requires learners to investigate causes, implications and ways of curbing this sort of crime and behaviour (Botswana Government, 2007a). However, although the curriculum developers have sought to separate moral from religious topics, they have curiously included *Botho* in the RE (rather than ME) syllabus under the heading of 'public virtues' (Botswana Government, 2007b, p. 5). Clearly, there is still some work to be done in differentiating between which topics ought to be covered in RE and which in ME.

Examining the current ME syllabus in some detail it is evident to see the influence of ME scholarship on its design. In particular, Kohlberg's (1969) thesis that children's moral maturity increases as they grow older has informed the syllabus. The preamble of the revised ME syllabus contains direction to teachers on how to approach the subject. For example, the syllabus states that:

> The way people reason about moral situations becomes more and more complex as they grow older. Therefore what determines the level of moral development of a person is not a particular action he or she judges to be right, but their reasons for so judging. (Botswana Government, 2007a, p. iii)

The syllabus has attempted to adopt a liberal, anti-authoritarian and non-judgemental approach to ME. This, too, is congruent with contemporary views that, in a plural world, the school should explore a range of worldviews as part of the child's education (Valk, 2007). In order to ensure that teaching in ME does not favour a particular worldview, religious or not, the Botswana syllabus promotes a 'value neutral' approach to encourage teachers to become 'neutral facilitators' in the classroom. The syllabus goes on to note that:

> In the Value Neutrality approach, the teacher ought not to provide authoritative answers. The teacher leads learners to discuss controversial issues as a neutral facilitator and encourages quality discussions. They [teachers] must demonstrate to pupils how moral arguments are conducted and moral conclusions made. (Botswana Government, 2007a, p. iii)

The 'values clarification' approach, originally espoused by Raths *et al.* (1966) has been adopted in Botswana. In spite of criticism—for example, that it has no effect on value priorities, dogmatism or preferences for traditional or emergent values (Lockwood, 1978)—this approach provides a useful classroom strategy for dealing with moral issues, as outlined in the Botswana ME syllabus:

> In the Values Clarification approach, the teacher need not transmit values, but should rather help learners to reflect on what they value and come up with personal and independent opinions and a clearer direction of what they have to do. The process involves choosing, prizing and acting. (Botswana Government, 2007a, p. iii)

The implications of the secular pedagogy for teachers of ME in Botswana should be noted. In a country where Christianity accounts for over 80% of the population (Haron & Jensen, 2008) and where the majority of current ME teachers were trained as RE specialists, serious questions need to be asked about the possibility of teachers approaching ME from a neutral standpoint, as national policy dictates. While no study has yet investigated ME teachers' experiences of and attitudes to this issue in Botswana, studies in other countries—for example in England (McCreery, 2005)—point to the difficulties teachers face in implementing a secular approach to ME after having previously conducted confessional forms of RE.

Part of the problem is that the relationship between ethics and religion, as between ME and RE, is both complex and subtle. In addition, global and national plurality of beliefs and values provides a challenge for anyone teaching ME or RE. Every teacher will therefore need to come to terms with a diversity of moral and religious starting points. It is not at all impossible that in Botswana some ME teachers, particularly those trained in Christian theology and supported by their own personal convictions, might see little value in using a non-religious and value-neutral approach to ME. Instead, they may prefer the use of Christian moral values, with which they are both comfortable and familiar, over a secular approach. The situation in Botswana is not unlike that in Nigeria, where there is an ongoing struggle to implement a secular ME syllabus widely in schools because religion (mainly Christianity and Islam) and morality have, for over a century, been inextricably linked (Obidi, 1993).

Conclusion

The paper has explored the three main phases through which ME has evolved in Botswana since pre-colonial times. It has noted, for example, the role that initiation schools played in the inculcation of traditional moral values. It has also demonstrated the impact of Christianity on indigenous ME during the colonial period and for much of the post-independence period. Finally, it has shown how a secular approach to ME, combined with the introduction of ME as a stand-alone subject, is beset by challenges, some practical and others ideological. There are a number of conclusions and implications to be drawn from this analysis.

The first is that a secular approach to ME in a religiously and culturally pluralistic society seems to be the fairer option, in keeping with Botswana's democratic aspirations. Promoting the values of one religious tradition in a country with people belonging to a number of different faith traditions would contradict the spirit of equality and diversity entrenched in the country's constitution.

Second, while a secular approach to ME has on the whole been lauded, it remains to be seen whether religiously-committed teachers or those trained to teach RE are able to make the transition to teaching ME from within a secular paradigm. Careful preparation of teaching materials, of student and in-service teachers and of educational managers needs to precede such a shift. In order to bridge the gap between the implementation of a new ME syllabus, it is recommended that an additional teaching qualification course in ME be made mandatory for those teachers not professionally trained in the subject. Included in such a course should be an explicit module about the difference between how ME is taught as part of the RE component of a school's curriculum and how it ought to be taught as a component of the core subject ME within a secular framework.

Finally, there is much to be said for reframing ME as a compulsory, stand-alone, core subject within secondary schools. The subject is bound to become more highly regarded and more central to young people's studies. For this to occur, however, careful attention needs to be paid to subject content and evaluation and how the subject fits with the constitution and human rights framework of the country. Over time the subject should become properly resourced with appropriate expertise developed. A subject adequately resourced and approached with appropriate pedagogies has the potential to help young people deal with the multiple moral issues they face in a rapidly modernising society such as that of Botswana. These include the ability to deal with current social and personal challenges such as HIV/AIDS infection and the stigma attached to the disease, as well as violence to self and others.

Acknowledgements

With sincere thanks to Sharlene Swartz, two anonymous referees and three staff members in the Religious Education Department at the University of Glasgow—Roisin Coll, Leon Robinson and Leonardo Franchi—for their constructive comments and editorial suggestions which have considerably improved this paper. However, all errors and omissions are mine.

Notes

1. These are the BaKgatla, BaKwena, BaLete, BaNgwato, BaNgwaketse, BaRolong, BaTawana and BaTlokwa.
2. So-called 'minor' tribes include BaHerero, BaSarwa, BaHambukushu, BaYei, BaKalanga, BaKgalagadi, Afrikaner, BaTlharo and BaHurutshi. This classification is resented by members of these tribes who are actively campaigning for a repeal of a law justifying this classification (Nyati-Ramahobo, 2008).
3. As part of the consultation process the SNCE used a number of methods to collect opinions and ideas. These methods included institutional visits, analysis of written and oral submissions on the proposed reform guidelines, reading of published research and policy studies and educational visits to a number of countries both within and beyond Africa.

References

Adeyemi, M. (2007) Botswana: an example for teaching the concept of interdependence, *Universitas*, 3(1), 1–9.

Amanze, J. (2002) *African traditional religions and culture in Botswana* (Gaborone, Botswana, Pula Press).

Awino, J., Mmolai, S. & Dinama, B. (2004) Some perceptions about the separation of religious education and moral education in Botswana schools, *Mosenodi: Journal of the Botswana Educational Research Association*, 12(1 & 2), 82–89.

Balogi, K. (2004) At the crossroads: family, youth deviance and crime control in Botswana, *Pula: Botswana Journal of African Studies*, 18(1), 77–87.

Botswana Government (1977) *'Education for Kagisano': report of the National Commission on Education* (Gaborone, Government Printer).

Botswana Government (1993) *Report of the [Second] National Commission on Education* (Gaborone, Government Printer).

Botswana Government (1994) *The revised national policy on education* (Gaborone, Government Printer).

Botswana Government (1996) *Three-year junior secondary syllabus: religious education* (Gaborone, Government Printer).

Botswana Government (1998) *Three-year junior secondary syllabus: moral education* (Gaborone, Government Printer).

Botswana Government (2007a) *Three-year junior secondary syllabus: moral education* (Gaborone, Government Printer).

Botswana Government (2007b) *Three-year junior secondary syllabus: religious education* (Gaborone, Government Printer).

Botswana Press Association (2008, March 11) Botswana: tourism contributes 16% to GDP, *The Voice*. Available online at: http://allafrica.com/stories/200803110721.html (accessed 12 May 2010).

Brown, J. (1921) Circumcision rites of the Becwana tribes, *Journal of the Royal Anthropological Institute of Great Britain and Ireland,* 51(July–Dec), 419–427.

Canada Government (1991) *Shared values: the Canadian identity* (Hull, Canada, Ministry of Supply and Services).

Clarke, L. (1999) *Moral education* (Gaborone, Botswana, Pyramid Publication).

Conteh, C. (2008) Rethinking Botswana's economic diversification policy: dysfunctional state-market partnership, *Commonwealth and Comparative Politics,* 46(4), 540–554.

Denbow, R. & Phenyo, T. (2006) *Culture and customs of Botswana* (Westport, CT, Greenwood Press).

Gaie, J. & Mmolai, S. (2007) *The concept of Botho and HIV/AIDS in Botswana* (Nairobi, Kenya, Zapf Chancery).

Greer, J. E. (1983) Religious and moral education: an exploration of some relevant issues, *Journal of Moral Education,* 12(2), 92–99.

Haron, M. & Jensen, K. (2008) Religion, identity and public health in Botswana, *African Identities,* 6(2), 183–198.

Hirst, P. (1974) *Moral education in a secular society* (London, University of London Press).

Iheoma, E. (1985) Moral education in Nigeria: problems and prospects, *Journal of Moral Education,* 14(3), 183–193.

Kohlberg, L. (1969) Stage and sequence: the cognitive-developmental approach to socialization, in: D. Goslin (Ed.) *The handbook of socialization theory and research* (Chicago, Rand McNally), 347–480.

Kohlberg, L. (1974) Education, moral development and faith, *Journal of Moral Education,* 4(1), 5–18.

Kumo, W. (2009, 3 May) Foreign exchange reserves during economic crisis, *American Chronicle.* Available online at: http://www.americanchronicle.com/articles/printFriendly/101155 (accessed 26 June 2009).

Lindfield, D. (1986) Trends in religious education. Paper presented at a workshop on *Botswana's development in the past 20 years of independence,* Gaborone, University of Botswana, June 16–20.

Lockwood, A. (1978) The effects of values clarification and moral development curricula on school-age subjects: a critical review of recent research, *Review of Educational Research,* 48(3), 325–364.

Mafirakurewa, M. (2009, February 6) Botswana: 9000 jobs for citizens, *Africa News.* Available online at: http://www.africa-interactive.net/site/list_message/18354 (accessed 11 May 2010).

Makgala, C. (2009, June 5) The Bakgatla-baga-Kgafela's initiates' rites and the modern society, *Mmegi Newspaper.* Available online at: http://www.mmegi.bw/index.php?sid=7&aid=21&dir=2009/June/Friday5 (accessed 26 April 2010).

Marope, O. (1996) The impact of educational policy reforms on the distribution of educational outcomes in developing countries: the case of Botswana, *International Journal of Educational Development,* 16(2), 157–171.

Matemba, Y. H. (2005) Multi-faith religious education in Botswana, *Religious Education,* 100(4), 404–424.

Matemba, Y. H. (2009) Religious education in the context of sub-Saharan Africa: the Malawian example, *British Journal of Religious Education,* 31(1), 41–51.

Mautle, G. (2001) Formal education among the peoples of Botswana before 1840, *Mosenodi: Journal of the Botswana Educational Research Association,* 9(2), 25–33.

Mbiti, J. (1991) *Introduction to African religions* (Oxford, Heinemann).

McCreery, E. (2005) Preparing primary school teachers to teach RE, *British Journal of Religious Education,* 27(3), 265–277.

McKinney, S. & Conroy, J. (2007) Religious education in Scotland, in: E. Kuyk, R. Jensen, D. Lankshear, E. Loh Manna & P. Schreiner (Eds) *Religious education in Europe: situation and current trends in schools* (Oslo, IKO Publishing), 223–230.

Mgadla, P. (1989) *Missionaries and Western education in the Bechuanaland protectorate 1859–1904: the case of Bangwato* (Gaborone, University of Botswana).

Nyati-Ramahobo, L. (2008) *Minority tribes in Botswana: the politics of recognition.* Available online at: http://www.unhcr.org/refworld/docid/496dc0c82.html (accessed 26 April 2009).

Obidi, S. (1993) A study of the reactions of secondary grammar school students to indigenous moral values in Nigeria, *Journal of Negro Education,* 62(1), 82–90.

Pandey, S. & Moorad, F. (2003) The decolonisation of curriculum in Botswana, in: W. Pinner (Ed.) *International handbook of curriculum research* (Mahwah, NJ, Lawrence Erlbaum Associates), 453–474.

Pastoral Institute of Eastern Africa (1974) *Christian living today: Christian religious education for secondary schools—a study of life themes* (London, Geoffrey Chapman).

Purpel, D. (1998) Values education in the United States of America, in: J. Stephenson, L. Ling, E. Burman & M. Cooper (Eds) *Values in education* (London, Routledge), 195–205.

Ramsay, J., Morton, B. & Mgadla, P. (1996) *Building a nation: a history of Botswana from 1800 to 1900* (Gaborone, Botswana, Longman).

Raths, L., Harmin, M. & Simon, S. (1966) *Values and teaching* (Columbus, OH, Charles E. Merrill).

Renwick, N. (2007) Global society's response to HIV/AIDS: Botswana's experience, *Global Society,* 21(2), 133–153.

Scanlon, C. (2000) *Moral education: Form 1* (Gaborone, Botswana, Longman).

Schapera, I. (1978) *Bogwera: Kgatla initiation* (Gaborone, Botswana, Phuthadikobo Museum).

Simuchimba, M. (2001) Religious education in a 'Christian nation': the case of Zambia, *British Journal of Religious Education,* 23(2), 107–116.

Tsayang, G., Sheldon, W. & Ndobochani, M. (2006) *Report of a panel on 'passion killings'.* Available online at: www.botsoc.org.bw/reports/passion-killings.htm (accessed 26 April 2009).

Valk, J. (2007) Plural public schooling: religion, worldviews and moral education, *British Journal of Religious Education,* 29(3), 273–285.

Van Deventer, K. (2009) Perspectives of teachers on the implementation of Life Orientation in Grades R–11 from selected Western Cape schools, *South African Journal of Education,* 29(1), 127–145.

Zeppel, H. (2007) *Indigenous ecotourism: sustainable development and management* (Reading, UK, Commonwealth Agricultural Bureaux International).

Moral education in a post-conflict context: the case of Burundi

Herménégilde Rwantabagu

University of Burundi, Burundi

Burundi, like the rest of the Great Lakes region, has been shaken by widespread inter-communal divisions and violent conflict. It is commonly believed that the troubled history of Burundian society has been due to the lack of a consistent moral dimension in school curricula. It is this obvious gap that the Catholic Church, through its Moral Education Programme initiated in 2005, sought to address. The new curriculum, implemented gradually in Burundian schools, takes inspiration from traditional human values. The programme is community- and situation-based and places emphasis on an active-participatory approach, in which learners try to appropriate and apply in their daily lives the moral precepts they learn in the classroom. In a post-conflict context, it is incumbent upon parents, teachers and the churches (preferably in partnership) to erect the pillars of peace by teaching moral values to the younger generation which will prevent future conflict.

Introduction

Within the African context, the post-colonial states, including Burundi, have been characterised by intra-national crises and inter-ethnic conflict. On the one hand, the situation may be explained by the failure of the ruling class to establish democratic institutions and to ensure social and economic justice for all (Rwantabagu, 2001). On the other hand, it is commonly believed that the gradual loss of peace-enhancing moral values has been a major contributing factor. The loss of moral values can be attributed in part to Burundi's tumultuous history of power, colonisation, domination and conflict.

In the traditional setting, political power rested in an hereditary monarch who ruled the country in collaboration with a corps of wise elders, the Bashingatahe, as representatives from the Hutu and Tutsi ethnic communities (Ntahombaye *et al.*, 1999, p. 27). During the colonial period (1899–1916 by Germany and then 1916–1962 by Belgium), executive power at the highest level lay in the hands of the colonisers. The achievement of independence in 1962 and the subsequent abolition of the monarchy in 1966 set the stage for rivalry between the Hutu and Tutsi élites, who vied for political position and economic privilege. These inter-communal divisions in Burundi have been exacerbated by the ethnocentric conception of power and the gradual radicalisation of the élite. This plunged the country into a succession of intra-national clashes, the loss of countless human lives and, since 1993, the massive displacement of parts of the population as internal or external refugees.

At the cultural level, the colonial experience resulted in the gradual replacement of traditional value systems with foreign value systems. These values have undermined the ethical foundations of Burundian society that guaranteed peace and harmony between individuals and between various ethnic members of society. Hence, as Kagabo (1994) has remarked, there has been a 'reversal of moral values' (p. 84) whereby such constructive attributes as honesty, solidarity, respect for human rights and reverence for life have lost ground in favour of negative ones such as injustice, egocentrism, violence and exclusion as a way of life, thus paving the way for lawlessness and destructive behaviour, particularly among the younger generation. However, in a study conducted by Ntahombaye *et al.* (1996) it was shown that Burundian youth arc aware of the significance and importance of traditional and contemporary moral values, although frequently failing to act on them. (In this regard see Swartz pp. 305–327, in this issue.)

Since the genocide of 1995, there have been complex and protracted negotiations between the conflicting parties, finally resulting in a power-sharing agreement and democratic elections in 2005. While the completion of the peace process and the integration of former rebel combatants into the national armed forces has, de facto, ended the sound of gunfire in the hills and villages, the scars of war have not yet healed in the hearts and minds of the people. The implication of this is that the 'institutional' peace that has been achieved remains a fragile and delicate edifice that needs to be strengthened by a well-grounded moral and social education programme that takes inspiration from the principles of traditional pedagogy, as emphasised by the 1994 UNESCO-sponsored national colloquium on a culture of peace in Burundi (UNESCO, 1994, p. 20).

In describing moral education in a post-conflict context, this article argues that the deep inter-communal clashes and divisions Burundi has undergone are due to a crisis of moral values and the collapse of traditional values in society. This is dealt with in the first part of the paper by paying attention to the nature of traditional values and their subsequent erosion. In the second part of the paper, an insider perspective on moral education is offered, calling attention to the need for partnership between family, school and community in future moral education endeavours. It also showcases how a new curriculum offered by the Catholic church in Burundi has the potential to revitalise moral education and contribute to healing the deep scars of the past.

Traditional approaches to moral education in Burundi

In traditional Burundian society, youth moral education was of paramount importance as an imperative for social integration and the perpetuation of cultural traditions. Hence, the homestead, with the backing of the community, constituted a 'wall-less school' (Rwantabagu, 2003, p. 8). As a Burundian saying goes, 'giving birth to a child is easy; what is arduous is educating him or her'. Parents therefore have always had a high level of awareness about their educational responsibilities to shape the character of children from a young age. In this respect, care was taken to follow the idiom '*Igiti kigororwa kikiri gito*', which means that you can give shape to a tree or person when it is still young.

Hence, the child was taught early about essential rules of conduct within the community. He or she learnt 'decency' of speech and behaviour and respect for parents and elders. In early adolescence, he or she learnt that natural impulses had to be curbed in the interest of the community and that a strict code of morality existed to secure this end, especially regarding the relations between the sexes, which were regulated by strict rules backed by severe sanctions. Thus, for the growing boy or girl, the moral code was written in the mind and heart, to become part of thinking and feeling. In Burundi as elsewhere in East Africa, indigenous education put emphasis on 'value inculcation and internalisation' (Ocitti, 1994, p. 44).

To secure this end, parents taught by counsel, proverbs and folktales, by setting a good example (Makarakiza, 1957, p. 79) and by adopting a virtuous deportment in their family and in their social interactions, as Kayoya (1971) demonstrates when he says: 'My father embodies the best human values; *Ubushingantahe*: sincerity, righteousness; *Ubumwe*: which is communicative solidarity; *Ubupfasoni* or nobility of heart; *Ubuvyeyi* as responsible parenthood; and *Ubuntu* or humanity that is respectful of human rights' (p. 41).

The method used in indigenous pedagogy was thus based on a strategy of dialogue in which all partners (parents and children) played their respective roles. Hence, the character of young people was slowly and imperceptibly moulded and impregnated with the prevailing social norms and values. Like the Greek '*arete*', the latter were not only internalised but also experienced and practised in everyday situations through deeds of patriotism, by protecting the weak and the elderly, by abiding by the laws of justice, respecting the rights of everyone and protecting the environment for the benefit of present and future generations. In this respect Senghor (1964) has observed: 'morality in Black Africa is active wisdom. It is not a catechism that is recited. It is a way of living that is realised in and by society and above all, within oneself' (p. 16).

The erosion of cultural values

Over the course of time, however, as Nkeshimana (2007) argues, 'the process of Westernisation has gradually eroded the binding power of traditional value systems as well as the social institutions which embodied those norms that shaped youth behaviour and ensured social harmony' (p. 121). Commenting on the decline of value consensus due to rapid social change, Cummings *et al.* (2001) note that 'in times of relative tranquillity, there is likely to be a high level of value consistency, but in times of rapid change, this consistency may break down' (p. 7). Burundi's history of a move from traditionalism, through colonialism (by Germany and Belgium) and then into a republic (by way of a number of military regimes) has been a period of rapid change.

Here I strongly argue that the advent of the colonial order, with the ethos that it entailed, has marginalised and weakened the local language, local cultural heritage and also the spiritual convictions of a monotheistic and God-fearing people.[1] During the colonial period, the institution of *Bashingantahe*, a body with immense and pervasive moral authority, was trivialised as an irrelevant anachronism. In addition, the Western model of schooling, by giving precedence to the cognitive while neglecting the ethical dimension of education has failed to produce men and women of humanity, who are unable to distinguish good from evil and to order their conduct accordingly. The process has led to what Kayoya (1971) calls 'the dehumanisation of man by egoistic inclinations' (p. 122).

In this respect, the loss of customary values such as temperance, decency in speech and social demeanour, selflessness, honesty, solidarity and, above all, the strict respect for human life, has degenerated into depraved inclinations such as alcohol and drug abuse, sexual promiscuity, violence, exclusion and intolerance on the basis of ethnicity, political or religious affiliation. Hence, as has been stressed by scholars such as Nizigiyimana (1999, p. 47), the political and social crises, civil wars and other evil tendencies generated by pseudo-modernity that have been a hallmark of many African countries, Burundi in particular, are above all, crises of moral values. The contemporary challenge is therefore, to seek efficient ways of rehumanising humanity through the revitalisation of fundamental values. In the case of Burundi, Adrien Ntabona (2009) emphasised that 'in order to overcome the present crisis, it is necessary to revive, learn and live by the fundamental moral values that are a characteristic of Burundian culture' (pp. 78–79).

The need for partnership between family, school and community in moral education

At all times, the moral upbringing of the younger generation has been a daunting and challenging task given its vital importance. The enormity of the task was such that no one agent could successfully undertake it alone. In Burundian traditional society, it was believed that education was too important to be left to parents alone. This is evident in the popular saying: '*Umwana si uwumwe*' meaning that 'a child does not belong to one person' but to the community. Therefore, as Jomo Kenyatta (1962) observed, 'in matters of social and moral education, any adult person may lend a hand' (p. 113). Indeed, since the community may be considered a wall-less school, each community member is expected to supplement the family's efforts in the upbringing of young people. The extended family and the public at large acted as harsh and objective judges and examiners of the behavioural standards attained by the young people in their communities. As a result of this community-based feedback to their parents, young people had the opportunity to adjust or to reinforce their action in the light of the evaluation received.

In the contemporary setting, one of the setbacks in moral education endeavours has been the decline of parental authority and indeed the abdication of the family as an agent of socialisation, which task schools alone could not fulfil. It has therefore become imperative, as Ndimurukundo and Mujawaha (1994, p. 8) emphasised, for the family to fully assume its educational responsibilities by joining hands with the school for more effective action, so as to achieve 'education for wholeness' by inculcating a kind of wisdom based both on 'knowing' and on 'being' (Rwantabagu, 1995, p. 9).

Revitalising the moral dimension in education: the new human values curriculum

In the wake of the deep social crisis, extensive violence and widespread destruction that Burundi has experienced for over a decade it is essential that moral education be revitalised. Furthermore, following UNESCO's (1945) dictum that 'since wars begin in the minds of men it is in the minds of men that the defences of peace must be constructed' these young minds are most readily to be found and accessed in schools. A moral education programme in school should therefore aim to restore ethical standards among the younger generation who have been most affected by the socio-political unrest in the country, both as victims and perpetrators of violence. After lengthy and national consultation facilitated by the Burundian government, between January 2004 and September 2005, all stakeholders involved—that is representatives of the Catholic church, teachers, school headmasters and parents—agreed on the urgent necessity to adopt and implement a moral education programme based on Burundian traditional values. The curriculum is school-based but includes elements of school–home partnership.

The curriculum, developed by the National Bureau for Catholic Education (2005), is currently in the process of gradual implementation in all the country's elementary and high schools as well as in teachers' colleges. The curriculum draws inspiration from the principles of Burundian customary pedagogy. The aim of the programme is to realise an 'all-round human education' based on the appropriation, by children and youth, of basic moral standards and their integration into daily life at school, in the family and in the community. The general orientation of the programme is based on what Noddings and Slote (2005) call the 'communitarian' approach. According to these authors, 'communitarians...hold, contrary to Kant, that it is only in relation to community values, traditions and good habits acquired in their context that we can become morally virtuous' (p. 342). They add that we become moral individuals only within a community with its tradition.

The content of this moral education programme is built around the following themes: respect for human beings and their rights and dignity; living in peace with others; tolerance and solidarity; justice and honesty; responsible sexual behaviour; a sense of social responsibility; protection of the natural environment; abiding by laws and regulations; and the peaceful resolution of conflicts. These principles are, by and large, inspired by the tenets of traditional education.

With regard to the teaching process in schools and colleges, the proposed pedagogical approach also draws on traditional learning practices. Since the objective of moral education is not 'to know', but 'to be', much emphasis is laid on interaction between the teacher and learners. The latter are encouraged to express themselves by relating their own experiences and their moral significance. On the other hand, teachers must ensure that lessons are lively, participatory and based on local and known realities. For this, teachers guide learners to select a number of moral values to focus on, depending on the perceived needs in the local community. In order to achieve this, the teacher, in consultation with parent representatives chooses and adopts one specific value as the 'Value of the Year' that will become a focal point for students as a guide to their behaviour and daily interactions. To enhance harmony and coherence among activities undertaken nationwide, a national coordination centre organises regular training and consultation seminars for head teachers and supervisors where experiences and approaches are shared and discussed constructively.

Lessons may take place within the walls of the classroom or outside, with occasional visits to hospitals or to homes of destitute elderly people as an outworking of the moral values of compassion and solidarity. Above all, the learners are encouraged to practise and 'live by' what they have learnt, because a moral value that is known but not practised is of no value.

The methodological implication of this reality is that instead of being directive, both parents and teachers shift the pedagogical emphasis to an active, participative and learner-centred moral education. In addition, the curriculum follows a constructionist approach by employing a 'day's events analysis' method that was practised in traditional education. This activity consists of an intimate and open exchange between teacher, parents and children on everyday problems experienced by, or likely to be experienced by, young people. Youth, in turn, are encouraged to discuss these issues in the classroom and at home, including alternatives for action and the consequences of each choice of action. Although, the impact of the curriculum has not yet been systematically evaluated, some anecdotal evidence exists that parents, teachers, education managers and learners have welcomed the curriculum, which, in some cases, has addressed controversial issues, such as school age pregnancy.

A further pedagogical device adopted to enhance the internalisation of positive human values among the young is peer education, particularly in high schools. In 2008, for example, there was a nationwide competition among high schools and colleges that encouraged theatrical performances highlighting changed moral values. In addition, sporting events have been purposefully arranged, with clear educational preparation, between youth from formerly hostile neighbourhoods so as to practise the principles of tolerance and dialogue, as taught in classroom lessons.

Conclusion

In Kiswahili there is a proverb that says 'Dawa ya moto ni moto', which means that for a serious illness there must be a strong remedy. In a context like Burundi, which has for many years experienced deep divisions, civil strife and serious moral degradation, it has been necessary to adopt a strong remedy so as to effect change and to rebuild consciences and communities.

The moral education curriculum initiated by the Catholic church and widely discussed in its form and in its substance by all stakeholders before its adoption and dissemination, has been hailed as a timely endeavour by teachers and parents. Its participatory and situation-based approach has been welcomed by learners and seems to be working in that there is a sense of changed behaviour (although this is not yet documented). Indeed, very little research has been undertaken so far on moral education in Burundi. An evaluation of the efficacy of the current programme is an urgent necessity. This and other gaps need to be addressed if moral education is to have a chance to fulfil its potential as an agent of change in post-conflict environments.

The partnership between the Catholic church, schools, parents and the community at large in the adoption of the programme, as well as in the follow-up to its implementation, may be a source of inspiration for other African societies that have experienced violence, social instability and moral disorientation. A moral education that takes account of traditional and cultural sensibilities can contribute to the genesis of a renewed society that is more decent and mindful of the dignity and nobility of people.

Note

1. According to the United States Department of State (2009) the religious affiliation of Burundi is estimated as being Roman Catholic 60%, Protestant 15%, indigenous religious groups 20% and Muslim 2–5%.

References

Cummings, W. K., Tatto, M. T. & Hawkins, J. (Eds) (2001) *Values education for dynamic societies: individualism or collectivism* (Hong Kong, Comparative Education Research Centre).

Kagabo, L. (1994) The Burundi crisis and the collapse of moral values. Paper presented at *UNESCO National colloquium on a culture of peace in Burundi: educational foundations and prospects*, Bujumbura, 14–17 December.

Kayoya, M. (1971) *In the footsteps of my father* (Bujumbura, Presses Lavigerie).

Kenyatta, J. (1962) *Facing Mount Kenya* (New York, Vintage Books).

Makarakiza, A. (1957) *The dialectics of the Barundi* (Brussels, Free University of Brussels).

National Bureau for Catholic Education (2005) *Human values education programme* (Bujumbura, Presses Lavigerie).

Ndimurukundo, B. & Mujawaha, M. (1994) *The role of the family in the promotion and consolidation of peace in Burundi* (Bujumbura, University of Burundi).

Nizigiyimana, D. (1999) What are values in education? *Au Coeur de l'Afrique*, 54(1), 45–64.

Nkeshimana, G. H. (2007) *Relevant education for Burundi* (Bujumbura, Renaissance).

Noddings, N. & Slote, M. (2005) Changing notions of the moral and of moral education, in: N. Blake, P. Smeyers, R. Smith & P. Standish (Eds) *The Blackwell guide to the philosophy of education* (Oxford, Blackwell).

Ntabona, A. (2009) *Itinéraire de l'éducation en famille au Burundi* [Itinerary for family education in Burundi] (Bujumbura, Presses Lavigerie).

Ntahombaye, P., Gahama, J., Ntabona, A. & Kagabo, L. (Eds) (1999) *The Bashingantahe institution in Burundi: a pluridisciplinary study* (Bujumbura, Presses Lavigerie).

Ntahombaye, P., Rwantabagu, H. & Mukarabe, P. C. (1996) *Perception and acceptance of traditional values and their link with contemporary cultural values among young Burundians* (Bujumbura, UNESCO).

Ocitti, J. P. (1994) *An introduction to indigenous education in East Africa* (Bonn, Germany, Deutscher Verkehrs-Verlag).

Rwantabagu, H. (1995) The family and moral education in a changing world: the case of Burundi. Unpublished paper, The University of Burundi.

Rwantabagu, H. (2001) Explaining inter-state conflicts in Africa: the case of Burundi, *International Journal on World Peace*, 18(2), 41–53.

Rwantabagu, H. (2003) *Moral education and social harmony: traditional perspectives and present challenges* (Bujumbura, The University of Burundi).

Senghor, L. S. (1964) *Négritude et humanisme* (Paris, Editions du Seuil).

United Nations Educational, Scientific and Cultural Organization (1945) *Constitution*. Available online at: http://portal.unesco.org/en/ev.php-URL_ID=15244&URL_DO=DO_TOPIC& URL_SECTION=201.html (accessed 25 March 2010).

United Nations Educational, Scientific and Cultural Organization (1994) *Educational foundations and prospects*. Report of the National colloquium on a culture of peace in Burundi (Bujumbura, UNESCO).

United States Department of State (2009) *Report on international religious freedom—Burundi*. Available online at: http://www.unhcr.org/refworld/docid/4ae861534b.html (accessed 25 March 2010).

Post-conflict teacher development: facing the past in South Africa

Gail Weldon

Western Cape Education Department, South Africa

One of the priorities of societies emerging from identity-based conflict is to signal a new society, with new values that stand in stark contrast with the old. Education policy becomes a critical arena for highlighting these political values when schools, particularly teachers, are identified as key agents of social change. However, the legacy of the conflict, especially with regard to teacher identities shaped during conflict, is seldom taken into account. This paper argues that unless appropriate programmes of teacher professional development are put in place to open the space for teachers to engage with painful personal legacies of the past, the aim of transforming society through the education system has little chance of succeeding. Using South Africa as the case study, this article analyses the post-Apartheid history curriculum and discusses a teacher development programme, Facing the Past, which, it is argued, provides the necessary conditions for teachers to engage with the past in a way that enables them to integrate issues of moral and ethical decision-making into their teaching.

Introduction

On the 27 April 1994 the people of South Africa went to the polls in what has become thought of internationally as the 'miracle' elections (Morrow, 1994). However, while the elections of 1994 formally ended Apartheid, 16 years later, in 2010, the country still grapples with its traumatic legacy. Schools and universities, as microcosms of society, reflect these tensions. In the years since Apartheid ended, there have been a number of high profile racially motivated incidents in schools and universities. In one incident, which occurred at the University of the Free State, four white male students were videotaped putting black workers through an 'initiation', which apparently included making them eat food that had been urinated on (South African Press Association, 2008). What is significant is that these young men did not experience Apartheid directly. They were displaying attitudes and values learned from the 'socialising agencies' (Jansen, 2009a, p. 331) they had been exposed to: their families, school, church and the communities in which they grew up.

This incident, along with two recent studies (Jansen, 2009b; Weldon, 2009) illustrates that insufficient attention has been paid by educational researchers to the traumatic legacy of conflict. Drawing on both these studies that describe a new field—post-conflict pedagogy and curriculum studies—this article focuses on teacher identities in post-Apartheid South Africa. By considering the context of history teaching in South Africa, it raises the question of appropriate professional development for teachers who are expected to teach in the midst of new political visions in a post-conflict society.

South Africa's history of conflict

Apartheid South Africa was a society based on legalised and institutionalised segregation aimed at 'the protection of Afrikanerdom, white power and the white race' (Beinart, 1994, p. 141). A series of laws put in place during 1949 and 1954 formalised segregation. The Population Registration Act (Republic of South Africa [RSA], 1950a) classified people as belonging to different 'races'; the Prohibition of Mixed Marriages Act (RSA, 1949) banned marriages across the racial divides; the Group Areas Act (RSA, 1950b) identified separate residential areas; and the Separate Amenities Act (RSA, 1954), in theory, provided equal separate amenities such as park benches, beaches, and toilets for the different 'races'. Apartheid's authoritarian system of racial domination, ethnic segregation and discrimination on the basis of race, permeated all aspects of life, resulting in deep-rooted racialised identities.

Erwin Staub (2003), in relation to the Rwandan genocide, describes how this occurs in practice. It has transferable insights for South Africa. Racial segregation enables lines to be drawn between 'us' and 'them' resulting in the devaluation of whole groups. Whole group devaluation then serves to justify discrimination, while discrimination, in turn, maintains devaluation. Consequently, moral values and principles are no longer applied by those devaluing to those devalued. In South Africa, moral, ethical and religious values were distorted to legitimise the Apartheid state. The result was a society mired in deep socio-economic inequalities and moral injustices.

At the centre of these injustices was the way in which education was employed. Education became a tool for division and repression (Kallaway, 1984). Education policy was 'based on the principles of trusteeship, non-equality and segregation' (Ashley, 1989, p. 19). The curriculum deliberately inculcated notions of superiority (of whites) and inferiority (of blacks). Education for black South Africans aimed to prepare them to accept inequality as part of the unchallenged order (Christie & Collins, 1984). Whites, in being educated to superiority, were also victims—of a 'deficient education system based on white supremacy' and of 'lies and deceit' (Jansen, 2009a, p. 329).

The reality for the majority of South Africans was an insidious daily humiliation. Lindner (2006a) defines humiliation within the modern human rights context, as 'the enforced lowering of any person or group by a process of subjugation that damages their dignity; "to be humiliated" is to be placed in a situation...in a demeaning and damaging way' (p. xiv). Perpetrators are also psychologically damaged and may experience humiliation. Judith Herman, a trauma researcher, offers evidence that shows how people who commit atrocities fail to get rid of their post-traumatic symptoms. Rather, 'they seem to suffer the most severe and intractable disturbances' (Herman, 1997, p. 185). Studies on perpetrators have found that many people who engage in intense violence against others are deeply affected by their own actions—the act of killing results in psychological and spiritual wounds (Staub *et al.*, 2005) and, for many, a deep sense of humiliation (Lindner, 2006b). In the South African post-Apartheid context these effects are fully experienced, resulting in a complex and traumatic legacy.

Ariel Dorfman (2004), writing about Eastern Europe and Rwanda, speaks of the 'dilemmas that flood societies' (p. xiii) after internecine conflict, when survivors have to find a way of living with those who have killed their families and trust has to be restored to communities. Similarly, South Africa is still struggling to find closure on many issues relating to the past; partly, it has been suggested, because the wounds are still raw and partly because of the difficulty in acknowledging the depths of the trauma (Ramphele, 2008). This struggle for closure becomes evident not only in continued racism, but also in the violent nature of protests against poor service delivery, poor wages, university fee increases and in the widespread xenophobic attacks that occurred in South Africa in 2009. Staub (2003) notes that many people who have been victimised themselves become violent. This ongoing violence in South Africa can be seen to be a legacy of an unresolved past, particularly of the brutality and violent repression of mass resistance in the 1980s.

The question that needs to be asked, therefore, is how, given the traumatic legacy of Apartheid conflict, can teachers shaped by the conflict become change agents for a new, democratic society? In 2002, a new national curriculum (National Curriculum Statement or NCS) was introduced in South Africa. The overall aim of the curriculum is to develop young people who 'will act in the interests of a society based on respect for democracy, equality, human dignity, life and social justice' (South Africa Department of Education, 2002, p. 1). To ensure the infusion of issues of human rights, social and environmental justice into all subjects, the work of the subject writing teams was monitored and guided by members of the South African Human Rights Commission (Keet & Carrim, 2006; Weldon, 2009). History was considered to be one of the most important subjects for delivering a values-based education—a subject that 'helps to empower an informed citizenry [and which]…may actually help sustain a more open, equitable and tolerant society' (Asmal, 2004, p. xi).

While expecting teachers to teach a values-based curriculum, none of the official teacher training programmes for the new curriculum engaged the dual legacies of identity-based conflict and a deeply unequal and divided society. Engaging these legacies is critical to supporting teachers to become agents of change in their schools and classrooms. The Facing the Past—Transforming our Future professional development programme for history teachers in the Western Cape was set up in 2003 in response to this gap.[1] It recognises that conventional, in-service professional development workshops for teachers will not be enough and employs an approach that engages both head and heart (see also Jansen, 2009a). The empirical data discussed in this paper were drawn from this project.

Each annual cohort of teachers is introduced to the methods and content of the Facing the Past programme in a four- or five-day workshop. A minimum of four one-day follow-up workshops are held during the year. The overall approach taken in Facing the Past is based on the scope and sequence of Facing History and Ourselves (Brabeck *et al.*, 1994, pp. 333–347; Schultz *et al.*, 2001, pp. 3–27; Tibbitts, 2006). This includes engaging with personal and group identity; historical case studies focusing on human behaviour and ethical decision-making (the Holocaust and Apartheid); and, critically for learners, 'choosing to participate'—encouraging young people to take on individual responsibility in their school and community. For many teachers, it is the first time that they will have had the opportunity to work so closely together with colleagues of different 'races' for an extended period of time.

Research approach and design

While educational research has failed to explore the implications of post-conflict traumatic legacies, there is a rich body of research, mainly in the field of psychology, which provides insight into the complexities of post-conflict states. The work of Volkan (2006a, 2006b), Lindner (2004, 2006a, 2006b), Staub (2003) and Staub *et al.* (2005) is particularly useful in understanding first-generation trauma along with the inter-generational transfer of traumatic knowledge. Post-Holocaust research is also informative, although it needs to be used with care. In post-Nazi Germany, unlike South Africa, the perpetrators and victims did not need to find a way of living together—Germans made sense of their past without the presence of surviving victims. The work of Mitscherlich and Mitscherlich (1975), Sichrovsky (1988), Bar-On (1989), Herf (1997), Jarausch and Geyer (2003) and Hoffman (2004) provides a range of insights into the way in which Germany came to terms with her past, both before and after reunification; the effects on children of perpetrators; and attempts to reconcile descendents of perpetrators and victims.

Besides these seminal empirical works, in examining the national processes that contributed to curriculum change, I drew on my personal experience as a participant researcher of curriculum development within South Africa. I was a member of the writing team for social sciences: history for Grades 1–9 and convenor of the history writing team for Grades 10–12. As convenor I had the overall responsibility for delivering an appropriate history curriculum within the national guidelines. I was also a co-founder of the Facing the Past programme and have co-facilitated teacher development workshops since 2003.

Data were gathered through analysing ideology and pedagogy in education policy documents; examining historical and political contexts; observing teacher evaluations during professional development workshops; and scrutinising a video-taped presentation made by learners on the Facing the Past programme for a school parent evening. All relevant data were transcribed in addition to detailed observation notes being made during workshops. Furthermore written teacher evaluations from workshops held in 2008 and 2009 were consulted, as well as notes made by independent observers during selected workshops. A total of 105 teachers, from all 'racial' groups and from a variety of schools from the four ex-education departments represented in the Western Cape (former 'white', 'coloured', 'black' and 'Indian'),[2] attended initial workshops between 2003 and 2008; 50 of these teachers attended multiple workshops.

Data were coded using open coding. Thereafter I read through the data sets several times looking for expressions of teacher identity and the legacy of Apartheid; grappling with changing identities in a society in transition; and the ways in which teacher identities filter curriculum knowledge in the classroom. The use of multiple sources of data, such as documents, workshop observation and individual and group interviews, helped to triangulate the findings.

I also reflected critically on my role as both national curriculum developer and as researcher within Facing the Past. In particular, I considered myself both insider and outsider within the history subject writing group (Jansen, 2009b, p. 34; Meyerson, 2003). The notion of insider is, in itself, very fluid. The group dynamics experienced during the writing processes, as group members, myself included, manoeuvred for various ideological positions, led to interesting shifts in my positions as insider and outsider. I was bringing several identities to the process, including that of a white, English-speaking South African, which further positioned me at times as an outsider. I attempted to apply the same critical self-reflection to my work with Facing the Past. One major evaluation of the programme conducted by Felisa Tibbitts (2006) has been valuable in that, amongst other contributions, it has allowed me the opportunity to compare and contrast some of my own findings against those of an external evaluator.

Facing the Past

It became clear at the first Facing the Past workshop with teachers in 2003 that the programme would need to provide teachers with the support needed to examine the ways in which the Apartheid past had affected them as individuals and as teachers. It was hoped that this, in turn, would help them to facilitate difficult conversations about the past with learners, in a way that would work towards a democratic future.

The work of John Paul Lederach—an internationally recognised practitioner in the field of conciliation and mediation—on the moral imagination provided a useful conceptual framework for this aspect of the Facing the Past programme. Lederach (2004, pp. 4–5) identifies four key elements of moral imagination. The first, which is central to the approach taken in the teacher workshops, is the capacity for people to imagine themselves in a web of relationships even with their enemies. The other elements are: the discipline to sustain curiosity; an eternal belief in the creative act; and the willingness to take a risk.

For the work of Facing the Past, the first key element of moral imagination is critical. Extending the capacity to imagine the web of relationships that holds society together is a desire to understand our enemies from their point of view—thinking in the presence of others, because the others are still present (Lederach, 2005). What is particularly pertinent to working within the legacy of identity-based conflict is the importance Lederach gives to understanding the past in order to comprehend the cycles of violent conflict. 'Lived' histories encompass the communal experiences that create and reinforce the stories of their collective lives and shared memories. The history of the formation of the group's identity, the construction of the group's future and its very survival are all about finding place, voice and story (Lederach, 2005).

Moral imagination does not see the past as something to be overcome, laid aside or forgotten in order to move toward a better future. Instead, the narratives that give meaning to people's lives and relationships must be told and the repetitive patterns acknowledged so that healing can take place (Lederach, 2005). People must attempt to discover where they have been, who they are, where they are going and how they will make this journey together. For teachers dealing with the legacy of internecine conflict, this provides a context not only for personal change but also for engaging in difficult conversations about the past and present with their learners.

The personal journey embarked on by Facing the Past teachers during the four-day introductory workshops is one of beginning to 're-story' their pasts—of uncovering and confronting the influences Apartheid had on them personally. One point of entry is a session called 'silent conversation'. Sets of extracts containing personal narratives of ordinary people from different 'race groups' living under Apartheid, are placed on sheets of newsprint. Participants move from one narrative to another, in silence, reading and writing personal responses to the narratives and to one another's comments. The session is drawn together in plenary. Many tell their own stories in the plenary session—some for the first time in a 'public' space.

Sharing narratives, both during this session and in the follow up workshops is, for many, a journey through cognitive dissonance (Weldon, 2005; Gorski, 2009), which begins to break down stereotypes and starts to build trust. Moving towards trust enables participants to start to imagine the former 'other' within their own web of relationships. It also involves Lederach's fourth element, risk-taking, as teachers share deeply personal stories.

Teachers and moral imagination

For teachers' involved in the Facing the Past programme the 'silent conversation' process allows those who find it difficult to talk about the trauma and hurt caused by the past, to express their feelings in safety and anonymously should they not want to share in the plenary session. By talking about what they or others have written, many also take a risk when they share their experiences and emotions in the plenary discussion. By the end of the workshop, and increasingly as the teachers come together over the years, they respond to the safety of the space provided, by talking more openly and more frequently to one another about Apartheid's legacy. Significantly, in the evaluation by Tibbitts, when teachers were asked in what ways the workshops had been valuable to them personally and professionally, the most frequently mentioned answer (from nearly half of the participants), related to increased self-awareness (Tibbitts, 2006, p. 17).

The comments that follow illustrate the various stages of some of the personal journeys through which teachers move. A number of comments indicate the extent to which humiliation experienced during Apartheid has been internalised. A black teacher wrote:

> I believe many Africans can identify with this. We still feel very much inferior to whites. (Black female, township school, Facing the Past workshop delegate, 2003)

There are those who remembered their own painful experiences and emotions when reading an extract. A coloured teacher shared with the large group that her father looked white but her mother had a darker complexion and how this affected an outing to the beach:

> My father once wanted to take us to a beach 'whites only'. We got there. The police stood at the turn-off. They would allow my father to go in, but not the '*meid* [domestic worker/ servant] and her kids'. All of us, including my father, cried all the way home. (Coloured female, urban black township school, Facing the Past workshop delegate, 2003)

For many white teachers the workshop experience results in growing self-reflection and engagement with emotions felt while growing up. A white male teacher wrote of his conflicting emotions when, as a child, he moved between an Afrikaans home environment and an English boarding school:

> I grew up in such a community [Afrikaans]. I was an 'insider' and 'outsider'. I had mixed emotions, mixed culture, mixed ideologies. I felt both humiliated and angry, as well as supremely embarrassed at how each community—Afrikaans, English, coloured and black—treated each other. It is still part of my consciousness. I was too often a bystander. I felt powerless and afraid. (White male, urban area affluent former white state school, Facing the Past workshop delegate, 2003)

Some teachers expressed the way in which their assumptions about 'the other' had been challenged:

> The stories of the 'white' teachers especially were significant. I think there are many generalisations that this group had no need to complain and that they all benefited from the old system. I think there is also a stereotype that those who did suffer must just get on with it, move on. What the Facing the Past workshops have done is to give us space and acknowledgement that our stories are powerful too. (Anonymous evaluation, Facing the Past workshop delegate, 2008)

Some teachers reported that the workshops helped them to have a greater awareness of their role in the classroom and responsibility towards learners. At the end of a Facing the Past workshop session during which the white activist Denis Goldberg—fellow accused at the Rivonia trial and sentenced to life imprisonment along with Nelson Mandela in 1964—spoke of his role in the struggle and experiences in prison, a black teacher commented:

> I was not always aware of my own prejudices prior to my participation in this project. I always saw myself as a victim of other people's prejudices and as generalisations such as

'whites are racists' never bothered me. But when Denis Goldberg told us of his involvement in the struggle against Apartheid I decided to re-look at how I view others. (Black male, rural township school, Facing the Past workshop delegate, 2008)

The comment of a white male principal-designate of a state school in the process of being set up to take learners from the existing, still largely segregated, primary schools in the area, reflected the first steps in the journey towards self-knowledge:

I needed to search my own heart for my own prejudices and my own thoughts and be confronted with my own inadequacies. ... (White male, rural state school in new area, Facing the Past workshop delegate, 2008)

Experience with the programme has provided evidence that personal change in a divided society is a complex process. The need for constant self-reflection was expressed by a teacher who has participated regularly in the programme since 2003. In the discussion session after Denis Goldberg's talk he made the following comment:

I have just realised how much I still teach resistance to Apartheid in a biased way...over the years I have tried to be unbiased in all of my teaching...but I now realise I have to work that much harder when it comes to resistance. (Black male, independent/private school, Facing the Past workshop delegate, 2008)

Evidence from the workshops suggests that the way to reconciliation and entrenching the values of democracy is not through forgetting the past or denying the ongoing racism that underpins South African society. After engaging with the issue of segregation in the USA in one session, a coloured teacher wrote of the connections he made with South Africa:

What was so noticeable is the deep hatred that is still hiding in some of us. It is unhealthy to be walking around with such feelings. What will happen if these feelings explode? It really worries me. We'll have to find a way to release our feeling in a positive way; otherwise it is going to affect us negatively for the rest of our lives. (Coloured male, rural former coloured school, Facing the Past workshop delegate, 2009, Author's translation from Afrikaans)

A black teacher wrote of the same session:

There were a lot of emotions—for some it did bring up bad memories. There is a lot to be done to get away [from] that hurt and hatred. All of us were victims of Apartheid, for some more than others. We as a group [teachers at the workshop] can't take blame for what happened but we have a chance here to improve and try to correct the past...to go and make a drastic difference in our communities. (Black male, rural township school, Facing the Past workshop delegate, 2009)

One of the participants who appeared to be most deeply affected by the experience of the four day workshops was a white Afrikaner male. In his final evaluation of the workshop, he wrote:

The fact that I was willing to share my deepest emotions with people I did not know four days ago, actually set me free. I realised I can talk about stuff without the fear of being labelled a racist or a privileged white man. (White male, rural state school in new area, Facing the Past workshop delegate, 2008)

The Facing the Past workshops reflect the conditions for reconciliation set out by Staub (2003), who highlights the importance of experience of the 'other', and Chaitin (2008), who emphasises 'joint dialogue through the sharing of personal stories and experiences connected to the traumas and through the creation of "safe spaces" for communication' (p. 35). She further maintains that while interpersonal reflection is important, the intergroup reflection is even more so. The teachers' comments reflect the personal journeys taken by many participants, critically in dialogue with 'the other'. Risks were taken in sharing deeply personal pain; in owning up to continued prejudice; and acknowledging that there is still deep hatred that needs to be confronted. One of the most poignant comments was that of the feeling of release expressed by the teacher who wrote of being set free by being able to 're-story' his life by acknowledging the past in the safe space created by fellow teachers.

Young people and border crossings

The ultimate aim of all teacher development in the Facing the Past programme is the cognitive, social and personal development of the pupil in the classroom. While the collection and analysis of data from young people taught by Facing the Past teachers is still in its early stages, one comment from a black pupil aged 15 in Grade 9 at a private school, when addressing a parents' evening in 2007, indicates that some learners are beginning to think in more complex ways about moral and ethical decision-making and the consequences of their behaviour:

> Studying the beginnings of Apartheid and Nazism in history brought me to the revelation that small comments can isolate people and can create an avalanche of hatred and violence. I realised how merciless I was being if I belittled someone when I talked behind their back or cut them off from 'my world' because they didn't 'belong'. I believe that history has opened up my way of thinking and understanding in all of my subjects. It is still difficult not to talk about people but I find it easier to speak out when friends talk about somebody and to be friends with someone 'outside' my group of friends. (Black female student, aged 15, affluent private school)

What is significant is this young person's recognition, not unlike that of the teachers who participated in Facing the Past workshops, that change is a process that needs continuous work.

Conclusion

Democracy in South Africa is fragile. While the Constitution guarantees basic political, civil and human rights, democratic practices depend on a culture that values and promotes these rights. Education cannot on its own be responsible for inculcating a democratic culture among youth, but schools and teachers do have a key role to play in preparing young people to become responsible citizens who value democracy. In a society undergoing transition, teachers may themselves have different views on the meaning of democracy and democratic practices. Teachers are not a homogenous body: they lived in different communities and had different experiences during the conflict years. Identities become deeply internalised, bolstered by group memories. One of the most fruitful fields of further research would be on how exactly the autobiographies, emotions and beliefs of teachers not only filter curriculum knowledge in the classroom, but impact on the way in which democratic values are taught through classroom interactions. Very little is known about this in divided societies.

I have used data from the Facing the Past programme because I believe that it is the only professional development programme in South Africa that takes teacher identities and the traumatic legacy of the past into account. There have been both internal and external evaluations of the programme and the evidence emerging from these evaluations and the workshop observations point to promising results in opening the way for teachers to make personal connections to a traumatic past. What has also emerged from this research is that personal change after internecine conflict is a long and complicated business.

Evidence from research conducted by Harland and Kinder (1997) indicates that lasting professional change comes only when there is value congruence between the policy message about 'good practice', or, in this case, required new values, and the teachers' own 'codes of practice' or values; that is, when policy intentions and teachers' beliefs about good practice or values coincide. In a post-conflict society this includes recognising and coming to terms with inherited attitudes and values and trauma of the past so that this self-knowledge can inform the change process towards new values. Furthermore, meaningful personal change in the post-Apartheid context cannot happen in isolation; it occurs within rebuilt 'relational spaces' (Lederach, 2005) in which meaningful interaction and the willingness to cross borders (Giroux, 1992) can take place. Teachers on the Facing the Past programme have only just begun their journeys of personal change. A moral approach to history teaching, such as that provided by Facing the Past, offers an important model for teacher development in the context of a society emerging from identity-based conflict.

Acknowledgements

The financial assistance of the South African National Research Foundation (NRF) towards this research is hereby acknowledged. Opinions expressed and conclusions arrived at are those of the author and are not necessarily to be attributed to the NRF.

Notes

1.   Originally a partnership between Facing History and Ourselves (FHAO), Boston, the Western Cape Education Department (WCED) and the Cape Town Holocaust Centre, it is currently a partnership between the WCED, FHAO and Shikaya, a non-profit organisation based in Cape Town, South Africa.
2.   For the purposes of understanding the composition of the group of teachers, the classifications in force under Apartheid have been used (RSA, 1950a). These are still used in many official surveys and documents for the purpose of ensuring employment equity. South Africa is also still a deeply racialised society and struggles to find ways of identification that are not race-based.

References

Ashley, M. (1989) *Ideologies and schooling in South Africa* (Cape Town, South Africa, South African Teachers' Association).

Asmal, K. (2004) Foreword, in S. Jeppie (Ed.) *Toward new histories for South Africa* (Cape Town, South Africa, Juta Gariep).

Bar-On, D. (1989) *Legacy of silence: encounters with children of the Third Reich* (Cambridge, MA, Harvard University Press).

Beinart, W. (1994) *Twentieth century South Africa* (Cape Town, South Africa, Oxford University Press).

Brabeck, M., Kenny, M., Stryker, S., Tollefson, T. & Stern Strom, M. (1994) Human rights education through the 'Facing History and Ourselves' program, *Journal of Moral Education*, 23(3), 333–347.

Chaitin, J. (2008) Bridging the impossible? Confronting barriers to dialogue between Israelis and Germans and Israelis and Palestinians, *International Journal of Peace Studies*, 13(2), 33–58.

Christie, P. & Collins, C. (1984) Bantu education: Apartheid ideology and labour reproduction, in P. Kallaway (Ed.) *Apartheid and education: the education of Black South Africans* (Johannesburg, Ravan Press), 160–179.

Dorfman, A. (2004) Introduction, in: E. Stover & H. M. Weinstein (Eds) *My neighbor, my enemy* (Cambridge, Cambridge University Press).

Giroux, H. A. (1992) *Border crossings: cultural workers and the politics of education* (London, Routledge).

Gorski, P. C. (2009) Cognitive dissonance as a strategy in social justice teaching, *Multicultural Education*, 17(1), 54–57.

Harland, J. & Kinder, K. (1997) Teachers' continuing professional development: framing a model of outcomes, *Journal of In-Service Education*, 23(1), 71–84.

Herf, J. (1997) *Divided memory: the Nazi past in the two Germanys* (Cambridge, MA, Harvard University Press).

Herman, J. L. (1997) *Trauma and recovery: the aftermath of violence—from domestic abuse to political terror* (New York, Basic Books).

Hoffman, E. (2004) *After such knowledge: memory, history and the legacy of the Holocaust* (London, Secker & Warburg).

Jansen, J. D. (2009a) When politics and emotion meet: educational change in racially divided communities, *Phi Delta Kappan*, 90(5), 327–332.

Jansen, J. D. (2009b) *Knowledge in the blood* (Cape Town, South Africa, University of Cape Town Press).

Jarausch, K. H. & Geyer, M. (2003) *Shattered past: reconstructing German histories* (Princeton, NJ, Princeton University Press).

Kallaway, P. (Ed.) (1984) *Apartheid and education: the education of Black South Africans* (Johannesburg, South Africa, Ravan Press).

Keet, A. & Carrim, N. (2006) Human rights education and curricular reform in South Africa, *Journal of Social Science Education*, 2006 (1). Available online at: http://www.jsse.org/2006/2006-1/keet-carrim-s-africa.htm (accessed 11 May 2010).

Lederach, J. P. (2004) The moral imagination: the art and soul of building peace. Keynote address to the *Association of Conflict Resolution Annual Conference*, Sacramento, 30 September. Available online at: www.acrnet.org/conferences/ac04/lederachspeech.htm (accessed 14 June 2007).

Lederach, J. P. (2005) *The moral imagination: the art and soul of building peace* (Oxford, Oxford University Press).

Lindner, E. (2004) The psychology of humiliation: Somalia, Rwanda/Burundi and Hitler's Germany. Unpublished PhD Thesis, University of Oslo.

Lindner, E. (2006a) *Making enemies: humiliation and international conflict* (Westport, CN, Praeger).

Lindner, E. (2006b) The classroom as a place for humiliating indoctrination or dignifying empowerment, in: D. R. Ganesan & A. A. Engler (Eds) *Humiliation in the academic setting: a special symposium issue of 'Experiments in education'* (New Delhi, India, Council of Educational Research).

Meyerson, D. E. (2003) *Tempered radicals: how everyday leaders inspire change at work* (Cambridge, MA, Harvard Business School Press).

Mitscherlich, A. & Mitscherlich, M. (1975) *The inability to mourn* (New York, Grove Press).

Morrow, L. (1994) Birth of a nation, *Time Magazine*, 9 May. Available online at: http://www.time.com/time/magazine/article/0,9171,980663,00.html#ixzz0ncWA8hh9 (accessed 19 May 2010).

Ramphele, M. (2008) *Laying ghosts to rest: dilemmas of the transformation in South Africa* (Cape Town, South Africa, Tafelberg).

Republic of South Africa (RSA) Parliament (1949) *The Prohibition of Mixed Marriages Act* (No. 55 of 1949) (Pretoria, Government Printer).

Republic of South Africa (RSA) Parliament (1950a) *The Population Registration Act* (No. 30 of 1950) (Pretoria, Government Printer).

Republic of South Africa (RSA) Parliament (1950b) *The Group Areas Act* (No. 41 of 1950) (Pretoria, Government Printer).

Republic of South Africa (RSA) Parliament (1954) *The Reservation of Separate Amenities Act* (No. 19 of 1954) (Pretoria, Government Printer).

Schultz, L. H., Barr, D. J. & Selman, R. L. (2001) The value of a developmental approach to evaluating character development programmes: an outcome study of 'Facing History and Ourselves', *Journal of Moral Education*, 30(1), 3–27.

Sichrovsky, P. (1988) *Born guilty: the children of the Nazis* (London, I. B. Taurus).

South Africa Department of Education (2002) *Revised national curriculum statement Grades R–9 (schools): overview* (Pretoria, South Africa, Government Printer).

South Africa Press Association (2008, February 27) Racist video slammed as 'barbaric', *Mail and Guardian*. Available online at: http://hades.mg.co.za/article/2008-02-27-racist-video-slammed-as-barbaric (accessed 11 May 2010).

Staub, E. (2003) Preventing violence and generating human values: healing and reconciliation in Rwanda, *International Review of the Red Cross*, 85(852), 791–806.

Staub, E., Pearlman, L. A., Gubin, A. & Hagengimana, A. (2005) Healing, reconciliation, forgiving and the prevention of violence after genocide or mass killing: an intervention and its experimental evaluation in Rwanda, *Journal of Social and Clinical Psychology*, 24(3), 297–334.

Tibbitts, F. (2006) Learning from the past: supporting teaching through the Facing the Past history project in South Africa, *Prospects*, 36(3), 295–317.

Volkan, V. D. (2006a) Trauma, mourning, memorials and forgiveness. Keynote address at *Memory, narrative and forgiveness—reflecting on ten years of South Africa's Truth and Reconciliation Commission Conference*, University of Cape Town, 23–27 November.

Volkan, V. D. (2006b) Large-group identity and chosen trauma, *Psychoanalysis downunder*, Issue 6. Available online at: http://www.psychoanalysisdownunder.com/downunder/backissues/6/427/large_group_vv (accessed 27 March 2007).

Weldon, G. (2005) Post-Apartheid South Africa, education and society, *International Journal of Historical Learning, Teaching and Research*, 5(1), 1–9. Available online at: http://www.centres.ex.ac.uk/historyresource/journal9/9contents.htm (accessed 17 May 2010).

Weldon, G. (2009) A comparative study of the construction of memory and identity in curriculum in societies emerging from conflict: Rwanda and South Africa. Unpublished PhD thesis, University of Pretoria.

'Deceptive' cultural practices that sabotage HIV/AIDS education in Tanzania and Kenya

Mary Oluga[a], Susan Kiragu[b], Mussa K. Mohamed[a] and Shelina Walli[a]

[a]Aga Khan University, Tanzania; [b]University of Cambridge, UK

In spite of numerous HIV/AIDS-prevention education efforts, the HIV infection rates in sub-Saharan Africa remain high. Exploring and understanding the reasons behind these infection rates is imperative in a bid to offer life skills and moral education that address the root causes of the pandemic. In a recent study concerning effective HIV/AIDS-prevention education, conducted in Tanzania and Kenya among teacher trainees and their tutors, the notion of *mila potofu* (defined by educators as 'deceptive' cultural practices) emerged as a key reason for educators' difficulties in teaching HIV/AIDS prevention education in schools and for high HIV infection rates. Since these cultural practices cause harm, and in many cases lead to death, they are of moral concern. This paper outlines some of these cultural practices identified by educators, including 'wife inheritance', 'sexual cleansing' and the taboo against certain foods, and discusses how these practices contribute towards HIV/AIDS vulnerability. It then offers recommendations for classroom-based life skills and moral education following Jean Piaget's theory of cognitive development in understanding how 'assimilation', 'accommodation' and 'adaptation' can help people discard *mila potofu* in a culturally sensitive manner.

Introduction

Sub-Saharan Africa (SSA) remains the region most heavily affected by HIV/AIDS worldwide. The United Nations Joint Programme on HIV/AIDS (UNAIDS, 2009) reported that of the 33.4 million people worldwide living with HIV/AIDS, two-thirds were from SSA. These latest HIV/AIDS statistics show that in 2008 the prevalence rate for adults aged between 15 and 49 was 7.8% in Kenya, 14.3% in Zambia, 16.9% in South Africa and 25% in Botswana. In Tanzania, prevalence was at 5.7% in 2007 (UNAIDS, 2009, p. 19). The principal mode of HIV/AIDS transmission in SSA is heterosexual contact (Kenya Demographic and Health

Survey, 2003) and more women are infected than men (UNAIDS, 2009). The overarching question is why the pandemic remains at such high levels despite numerous education and prevention strategies over the last three decades (Morrell, 2003). The answer to this question is important since it has the potential to reshape the strategies and content of HIV/AIDS interventions, especially for young people in colleges and schools.

Various authors have critically discussed the reasons behind HIV/AIDS prevalence in SSA. Parker *et al.* (2000) cite ecological contexts such as poverty, mobility and internal migration, seasonal work, social disruption due to war and political instability; Kiragu (2009) focuses on how gender inequalities, religion, stigma and discrimination and the historical background of colonialism impact on sexual decisions and behaviour; MacDonald (1996) reflects on multiple concurrent partnerships and intergenerational sex as key drivers; while others (Ahlberg *et al.*, 1997) discuss how traditional practices, such as circumcision with shared implements, are complicit in maintaining high rates of infection. Some of these factors, such as widespread poverty and social disruption, have resulted in poor education, a concomitant lack of knowledge of HIV/AIDS transmission and an inability to comply with some of the public health interventions advocated. These interventions include medical circumcision; treating sexually transmitted infections; adhering to a healthy diet for people on antiretroviral (ARV) drug treatments; obtaining and consistently using ARVs for prevention of mother-to-child transmission and for the care of those already infected; and consistently acquiring and using condoms. More recently, commentators such as Mbozi (2000), have added a further, frequently ignored, driver:

> There is no doubt about economic shortcomings as determinants of the high rate at which this deadly disease (HIV/AIDS) spreads. However, there is also evidence that some negative cultural beliefs, traditions and practices, which are deeply rooted in the social and sexual lives of most African ethnic groups, have also contributed to the transmission of the disease. (p. 75)

During a study that explored the challenges that educators (college tutors, teacher trainees and teachers enrolled in continuing education) faced in teaching HIV/AIDS and sexuality in school classrooms, the topic of 'deceptive' cultural practices was frequently raised. Educators called these practices *mila potofu* in Swahili, which they defined as those beliefs and activities practised within a community that present a danger to one's health, especially in the time of AIDS.

This paper focuses on these traditional and cultural beliefs and practices identified by educators in Tanzania and Kenya and interrogates their evidence as to how they impact on the fight against HIV/AIDS. The paper argues that addressing these deceptive cultural practices *sensitively* is both a moral obligation for educators and an important part of the moral education programme of a school, since failing to do so at all results in harm to others, while failing to do so sensitively does injustice to people's right to practise their culture. It suggests that while *mila potofu* poses obstacles for HIV/AIDS-prevention education, circumventing these practices in a sensitive manner is possible through what Piaget (1970) and others call 'assimilation', 'accommodation' and 'adaptation', which will be discussed in conclusion.

Research design and methods

The research study was conducted in Tanzania and Kenya in order to offer a comparative perspective on the experiences of teacher trainees and college tutors with regard to classroom-based HIV/AIDS education. In Tanzania, there were seven sites from which research participants were drawn. The first site was a primary school in the town of Turiani where the researchers taught a certificate course for teachers. Sites two to seven were teacher training colleges, three of which were urban—Arusha, Dar es Salaam and Iringa, while three were rural—Moshi, the Coastal region and Makete. With the exception of the college in Dar es Salaam (private and Muslim), all colleges were secular and run by the government. Colleges were chosen, in consultation with the Ministry of Education in order to obtain a mix of urban/rural and private/public institutions and to be representative of teacher training colleges in Tanzania. In Kenya, there were two sites, a primary school in the town of Kisumu and a secondary school in Nairobi where the researchers taught the same teacher certificate course as in Tanzania.

Permission to conduct this research was formally sought from the Ministries of Education in both Kenya and Tanzania. Once research permits had been obtained, researchers sought permission from institutional authorities to approach participants and then sought informed consent from individuals to be research participants. The overall research sample consisted of 137 individuals comprising 14 college tutors (including three college principals) and 123 teacher trainees (40 new teacher trainees and 83 teachers who were upgrading their qualifications). These individuals were purposively selected because they were either tutors or teacher trainees in subjects that incorporated HIV/AIDS education. There was an even number of male and female research participants.

Data were collected through individual interviews with college tutors and principals and through focus group discussions with teacher trainees at each of the nine sites. Teachers were divided into discussion groups depending on their regional and ethnic origin, for example, Luo, Luhya, Kikuyu and Kamba in Kenya and Northern, Southern, Central and Coastal regions in Tanzania. Each discussion group had both female and male teachers. Once teachers had identified *mila potofu* as a phenomenon that affected HIV/AIDS and sexuality teaching in the classroom, they were invited to conduct a focus group of their own regarding these 'unhelpful' or 'deceptive' cultural practices in their communities. Having completed this task they, in turn, provided feedback to researchers in focus groups. Interviews and focus group discussions were conducted in English and Swahili and were all digitally recorded and transcribed prior to analysis. Swahili transcriptions were simultaneously translated into English during transcription. Data analysis involved a thorough reading of the transcripts, and teasing out emerging *mila potofu.* These were further coded within similar themes such as 'taboo of talking about sex', 'nutrition', 'ceremonial rituals and myths' and 'cultural attitudes towards fertility and sexual intercourse'.

The moral implications of 'deceptive' cultural practices

Sithole (2003) aptly defines culture as a complex set of distinctive spiritual, material, intellectual and emotional features that characterise and define a society or social group. In the past 15 years, a growing number of African scholars have called attention to the role of myths and cultural beliefs surrounding nutrition and ceremonial and healing traditions that predispose people to the risk of HIV infection (MacDonald, 1996; Mbozi, 2000; Akinade, 2003; Sithole, 2003). These, and other scholars, report on widow inheritance (Luginaah *et al.*, 2005), sexual cleansing (Ayikukwei *et al.*, 2007), sex with virgins (rape) as a cure for AIDS (Leclerc-Madlala, 2002), mass, unsterile, male and female circumcision (Ahlberg *et al.*, 1997) and traditional styles of body scarification, tattooing and hair shaving using the same knife (Sithole, 2003). So while there is increasing recognition of the adverse effects of various cultural practices on levels of HIV infection, what was most interesting in our study was the clear way in which teacher trainees and college tutors identified particular practices as hindering HIV/AIDS education, called them by a historically understood name, *mila potofu*—'deceptive cultural practices'—and alluded to the moral importance of addressing them within HIV/AIDS education programmes in schools.

As Brandt and Rozin (1997) put it, 'HIV/AIDS has called attention to moral judgements and their impact on disease as few modern diseases could have' (p. 3). They alert us to the powerful role moral systems play in addressing matters of health and disease and argue that:

> All cultures seem to have complex and entangling moral and health beliefs. Moral conventions, at different times and places, have a significant influence on the framing of health and disease-related behaviours. We become more and more aware of the impelling fact that the morality-health link is both very important and little studied. (p. viii)

The empirical evidence provided below, aims not merely to describe these cultural practices, but to offer insight to educators on how they impact on people's 'local moral worlds' (Kleinman, 1999). Kleinman argues that traditions and customs are neither a matter of following pure habits nor of constant self-interrogation about how we make meaning of culture; rather the making of moral beings depends upon the way we place ourselves within local relationships—an area of crucial significance to teachers and teacher educators, as will be illustrated below.

Identifying *mila potofu*

Our research findings can be divided into four main areas. The first concerns the pervasive taboo regarding *talk about sex* between adults and children. This includes the reserved nature of educators in discussing issues related to sex and HIV/AIDS. In general, we found that according to teacher trainees, females and young children of both sexes were less likely to engage in discussions around sex. Second, there seems to be a plethora of myths and cultural beliefs surrounding *dietary practices* that impact negatively on women and children especially, and distort the educational quest for AIDS prevention and treatment. Third, a number of overt *ceremonial practices and myths* prevail that are directly harmful to those who are subject to them and place them at increased risk of HIV/AIDS infection. Fourth, various *sexual practices*, especially around the common practice of having multiple partners or extra marital partners, exist as cultural idioms of not only male virility but female fertility as well. These place women at heightened risk of HIV/AIDS infection. Each will be considered in turn.

The taboo of talking about sex

The key cultural belief and practice identified by educators as exacerbating the risk of AIDS infection in their communities was the taboo against speaking about sexual matters. In Kenya and Tanzania, not unlike other African countries, the discussion of sex with young people, especially girls, is seen as indecent, unhealthy and unacceptable (Campbell & MacPhail, 2002; Oshi *et al.*, 2005). One female college tutor summed up the taboo in personal terms:

> How does my husband start to talk about sex with my daughter? Where am I at that time? It is embarrassing. Oh no, what would he say, and how would she regard her father? A girl who listens to such talk is considered spoiled [immoral] in our community. There are only specific times like 'a kitchen party' [a pre-wedding occasion for brides] when they are taught, but it is women to women. Not before that. (Female college tutor, Tanzania)

During the course of the study, it was not uncommon for female teacher trainees to walk out of the room when matters of sex were being discussed. College tutors had a laissez-faire attitude to these 'walk outs'. One male college tutor expressed both exasperation and powerlessness:

> Really, these are grown-ups. Some of them are married people and I cannot force them to like what they do not want. If she feels it is against her culture, all I do is to respect that and let her walk out. (Male college tutor, Tanzania)

Furthermore, college tutors reported that parents were not in favour of education about sex and contraception in schools as they claimed it made their children 'immoral'. A male college tutor reported that:

> Talking about sex, especially with girls, is not allowed at all. It is not in our culture to do that, it is not allowed at all….Parents do not like it; they can even withdraw the child from the school.

At a teacher training college in Coastal region, Tanzania, teacher trainees complained that this taboo against talking about sex meant that both their own college tutors and the children they encountered in their classrooms were reticent (and frequently silent) about discussing issues related to HIV/AIDS. Upon hearing this feedback in an interview, a senior college official responded by saying that:

> HIV/AIDS does not provide teacher trainees with a certificate to discuss *mambo ya ajabu ajabu* [shocking/taboo topics]. We still have to remain decent!

At the same college, a male teacher trainee drew attention to how silence was an obstacle to behaviour change in both young people and adults. He commented that:

> We know that there are some things which our tutors do not want us to discuss in class because it is not allowed in the community. In this way, we miss a lot of truth. (Male teacher trainee, Tanzania)

When asked why children were silent during classroom discussion, a male teacher trainee reported that children 'keep a lot to themselves' because they feared the repercussions of talking about their experiences of sexual abuse. They feared the legal implications and also feared being seen to undermine their culture by speaking about sexual matters to adults:

> One girl told me, 'the way I see it, if I say that my grandfather is the one who did this to me [raped me] I will quarrel with my parents and they will not believe me'. (Male teacher trainee, Tanzania)

Numerous scholars capture the drift from open dialogue in sexuality matters to one of silence due to factors such as colonialism, patriarchy and religion (Foucault, 1976; Fine, 1988; Ahlberg, 1994; Kiragu, 2009). Indeed in pre-colonial Africa, communities such as the Gikuyu of Kenya (Kenyatta, 1938; Kiragu, 2009), Shona of Zimbabwe (Jeater, 1993) and Baganda of Uganda (Bryk, 1933) had a public, collective nature in which sexuality was addressed during initiation and ritual ceremonies. These cultural practices created a public discourse around sexuality, which stands in stark contrast to the silence surrounding the same in contemporary times as exemplified by the teachers in this study. Kiragu (2007, 2009) argues that silence among teachers is caused by the mixture of a lack of training in sexuality and HIV/AIDS education, cultural taboos of talking about sex, a fear of being seen as encouraging children to have sex and fear of being called 'obscene' or 'indecent' by using words such as 'penis' and 'vagina' with children. A Tanzanian college tutor summed up this helplessness. He related how a female teacher trainee had asked for help to know how to respond to children's abusive experiences. When asked by the researcher what advice he would give to this trainee he said, 'I, too, would not know what to do'.

The taboo against talking about sex operated at multiple levels. College tutors failed to speak to teacher trainees, who themselves struggled to speak to children, mainly for fear of offending parents or not knowing how to deal with the situation. In turn, children kept silent because of their fear of transgressing cultural norms and 'quarrelling' with parents, especially in cases where they reported abuse. This conspiracy of silence present in Tanzania and Kenyan cultures (and beyond) conspires to keep young people ignorant about the basic biology of HIV/AIDS and how various cultural beliefs, traditions and practices might be challenged in order to protect them from HIV/AIDS infection.

Nutrition—participation in dietary cultural practices

The second group of cultural practices that affected teachers' educational quest for HIV/AIDS intervention concerned cultural beliefs about food. Teacher trainees spoke about two main types of dietary beliefs of relevance. The first was the way in which certain cultural practices prevented children and women (including pregnant and lactating women) from accessing a balanced and nutritious diet, which resulted in malnutrition, stunting and sometimes illness and death. For example, certain cultural groups forbade women from eating protein-rich foods such as eggs, milk, fish and chicken. Other groups forbade pregnant and lactating women from eating fruits and vegetables, claiming that they are harmful to infants. More widespread is the practice of preventing women and children from eating until men have had their fill. As a result women and children were frequently inadequately nourished. A female teacher trainee from Tanzania explained:

> Many traditional cultures refuse women to take foods such as eggs, milk, fish and chicken. All these are foods rich in protein. In some cultures, it is only the men who are allowed to eat the chicken gizzard because it is believed to make the men *dume la mbegu* [virile like a bull with sperm] and a woman infertile. (Female teacher trainee, Tanzania)

A female tutor from the coastal region explained the voluntary avoidance of certain foods as a socio-cultural practice or due to unfounded myths. So, for example, some refused to eat vegetables and some fruits because they are seen to be 'lowly foods…food for the poor'. This belief, she explained, is especially common amongst tribes that have traditionally been hunters. She further elaborated how this affected HIV/AIDS intervention. In her experience of volunteering for home visits among people who were HIV-infected and on ARV treatment, she frequently encountered relatives of AIDS patients who actively discouraged them from eating vegetables, fruits and grains in spite of their affordability and high food value in boosting the immune system, due to this belief:

> They completely refused. They said that [eating]…leaves are not important. For them the leaves are for cows not for human consumption. (Female college tutor, Tanzania)

A similar story was related by a female teacher trainee in Kenya, who related that in her tribe, pregnant women are not allowed to eat eggs as it is believed they would give birth to bald babies. Such babies are said to cause poverty in the family. In poor communities, eggs are a main source of protein and are freely available and affordable. This cultural belief results in poorly nourished women and infants. It is made more complex by women themselves perpetuating the practice. During a classroom observation, a married male teacher trainee in Moshi, Tanzania related how his wife refused to eat eggs during pregnancy despite this being the only source of protein he could afford. He was desperate and asked:

> What am I supposed to do? I know eggs are very good for her and I can afford [them] because we keep a lot of chickens. But she refused—she said her mother warned her. (Male teacher trainee, Tanzania)

These beliefs and practices about fruit and vegetables as 'poor foods' and seeing protein-rich food as taboo, despite their ubiquity and importance, due to strong cultural beliefs and gendered positioning as regards food are difficult to address given the strong traditional bases for these beliefs. Due to social pressure to appear 'wealthy' in the community or through a strong belief in such myths or gender-priority, households in many African communities avoid eating, or prevent others from eating, readily available and highly nutritious food. The life chances of those who are subjected to, or partake in, these dietary practices are severely hampered, particularly if these people are HIV-positive. People infected with the virus require a healthy and nutritious diet in order to maximise the effects of treatment programmes. These dietary practices also have an effect on poverty alleviation, since people spend money on market-bought food instead of utilising the abundant supply of naturally growing food or foods that can be easily cultivated in vegetable gardens. One research participant recognised the drawbacks of eliminating good nutrition for the sake of cultural adherence:

> We must put aside our pride and ignorance and take advantage of nature's free gifts. Let us let go of those cultural practices that hold us back. (Female college tutor, Tanzania)

However, many more acknowledged that taking such a step, and helping children, families and communities to do so too, would be a difficult undertaking.

Ceremonial rituals and myths

Educators identified various ceremonial practices in the communities in which they lived that impact on AIDS education and prevention. These include circumcision, traditional healing and cleansing practices and other ceremonial rituals and myths (Ahlberg et al., 1997; Luke, 2002; Ayikukwei et al., 2007). During focus groups, teacher trainees and college tutors spoke at length about the 'dangers' of these practices largely due to the common feature of shared and unsterile instruments:

> When people visit traditional healers in order for their problems to be solved, a common treatment is for the traditional healer to make an incision into the client's skin into which medicine is rubbed. In most cases there is no guarantee that the instrument will be cleaned before the next client is offered the same service. Naturally, such a practice increases the risk of blood-to-blood HIV infection. (Female college tutor, Tanzania)

Another common belief is that HIV/AIDS can be cured through natural or herbal means. A Kenyan female teacher trainee related how the jackfruit is regarded as 'sacred' in her community and is used for healing purposes among sick people, including those suffering from AIDS. 'The belief is that if you eat the fruit for three months and rub the skin of the fruit on your body, you will be cured,' she related. As a result, she explains, people engage in risky behaviours with the belief that there is a cure and once they have undergone this ceremony they no longer take sexual precautions or get tested because they believe themselves healed.

A more commonly occurring belief is that of the virgin cleansing myth. A male Tanzanian teacher trainee summed up this belief:

> Many believe that AIDS is a result of a curse, resulting either from a personal offence to the spirits or mediated by a person who wishes harm. It is a belief among some communities that the remedy to escape such a curse is for the infected or cursed man to have sex with a virgin girl, usually under the age of twelve. Subsequently, the incidence of child

rape has increased in the communities among which this practice occurs, and this leaves these young girls HIV-infected. (Male teacher trainee, Tanzania)

Teacher trainees had many stories to tell regarding the virgin cleansing myth and spoke of friends and traditional healers being known to advise men to sleep with virgins as prevention and a cure for HIV/AIDS.

Another cleansing ritual involves a woman whose husband has recently died. Commonly known as widow inheritance, the practice is used in a number of ways: to ensure the widow is cared for; as a means to keep the wealth of the deceased within the family; and as a means to appease the spirit of the dead husband and prevent it from visiting and punishing the living (Luginaah *et al.*, 2005; Dilger, 2006; Ayikukwei *et al.*, 2007). In some communities, where death is considered a bad omen, a widow has to have sex with a stranger or even a 'mad' man so as to transfer 'the bad omen' to him. In this case, sexual cleansing or widow cleansing is seen as a sacred ritual. A 'cleanser' (a man who agrees to have sex with the widow) is identified, some of whom are paid for their services (Mulama, 2010). Widow cleansing perpetuates the HIV/AIDS epidemic since unprotected sex is had with multiple partners. A female Kenyan teacher elaborated further:

> The belief is that a woman who has lost a husband needs to be 'cleansed' before she can remarry. This cleansing ritual requires that a man other than the one who is to eventually marry the widow, to perform sexual intercourse with her. (Female teacher trainee, Kenya)

Furthermore, since this is seen as a temporary relationship meant to serve a ceremonial purpose, condoms are rarely used. Teachers spoke of children being born out of such encounters, evidencing unprotected sexual engagement. The implications for HIV infection are obvious. During focus groups and interviews, participants spoke animatedly of the various villages, regions and countries that participated in these cleansing practices, including Zambia, Mozambique and many parts of Kenya and Tanzania. They also discussed the consequences to women who failed to participate in the practice:

> Women who refuse to participate in this ceremony face the wrath of the extended family as they are blamed for being the cause of misfortunes in the family after refusing to be cleansed. (Female teacher trainee, Kenya)

> In other cases, the deceased husband's family chooses a random stranger, a homeless or sick person, to perform the ritual. (Female teacher trainee, Kenya)

> Some men who act as 'cleansers' have made this a professional practice and charge exorbitantly for the service. In some cases, desperate widows pay agents to get a 'cleanser'. (Male teacher trainee, Kenya)

A particular male teacher trainee told of how when there was competition for widows, cleansers would give items of clothing to an agent who in turn would ask a widow to randomly choose an item of clothing. She would be 'cleansed' by the man whose clothing item she had picked. While most teachers were visibly repulsed by this *mila potofu*, one male Kenyan teacher trainee seemed to be in support of it:

> I don't see why I should not be allowed to look after my sister-in-law in all ways possible. The one inheriting the widow, a brother or cousin to the deceased, has to perform the duties of a husband including providing and receiving conjugal rights. (Male teacher trainee, Kenya)

This teacher highlighted the related practice of widow inheritance rather than widow cleansing. Widow or wife inheritance is the cultural practice whereby relatives of the deceased ensure that the widow remains part of the family. A brother would marry the widow and, if he is already married, become polygamous to protect her and to keep her wealth in the family. In the presence of HIV infection, this practice has the potential for continuous infection from one member of the family to the next, leaving behind related orphans.

Cultural attitudes towards fertility and sexual intercourse

Although many of the cleansing rituals described above are sexual in nature, there are further cultural practices that focus on sexual intercourse and that have important ramifications for the transmission of HIV/AIDS. These include beliefs and practices about multiple partnerships, how to keep a sexual partner and other sexual practices which affect HIV infection. Trainees spoke frequently of the cultural icon of male virility and the common practice of having multiple partners or extra-marital partners. The idiom *ruath tho gi lum e dhoge* (literally translated from Luo as 'a bull dies with grass in the mouth') was commonly articulated amongst Luo teacher trainees in Kenya. They explained that the phrase meant that a man would not forgo multiple sexual partnerships or compromise his male ego to the possibility of contracting HIV/AIDS since such a practice was a sign of his virility and was applauded in the community. Appreciation of multiple sex partners was not only common among men. In Tanzania, it was reported that women from the Coastal region found it prestigious to have multiple sexual partners:

> These women are proud to have different children from different men, and take pride in talking about 'my seven children from six husbands'. (Female college tutor, Tanzania)

Whilst the issue of multiple partnerships as a sign of prestige is not unique to Africa (Kelly *et al.*, 2003), the way in which it is supported by traditional idioms makes it particularly problematic in the context of AIDS education. Another practice supported by a common expression in Tanzania regards the sharing of breast milk between a baby and a sexual partner. A female teacher trainee elaborated:

> *Baba na mwanae lazima wagawane maziwa* [the father and the child must share the milk]. One breast is for the father and the other for the baby. (Female teacher trainee, Tanzania)

Besides denying the infant adequate nutrition, this practice also carries the risk of infection or re-infection between the partners should the woman be HIV-positive.

In many communities, expectant women have been discouraged from having sexual intercourse especially in the last trimester of their pregnancy. Traditional midwives and mothers-in-law from a number of communities reprimand and ridicule women for having engaged in sex until the 'last minute' when a baby comes out covered in blood and 'a slimy membrane'. To avoid this embarrassment, women deny their husbands sex and in turn, men have extra-marital sex to satisfy their needs. This heightens their risk of HIV infection which later increases their marital partner's risk of infection when they resume sexual intercourse.

Teachers in Kenya mentioned two other cultural practices that increased the risk of HIV infection. Among the Maasai tribe, men are frequently stationed away from the community in search of greener pastures for their cattle. When these men are away, young women ('Maasai virgins') are sent to provide them with 'necessary services', which include food and sex. These young women are allocated to a group of men rather than to specific partners. The implication for HIV infection is obvious:

> When the Morans [Maasai warriors] are out there, they are protecting the community and so their well-being is important. All their needs have to be served. They are sent young virgins to satisfy their sexual needs in addition to carrying foodstuffs and water for them. (Male teacher trainee, Kenya)

Finally, a male teacher trainee in Tanzania related a discussion that he had had with his students (aged 9 to 12). The children told of a custom of grandfathers calling their granddaughters 'my little wife' and grandmothers calling their grandsons 'my little husband'. Traditionally, these pet names are regarded as endearing references with no sexual overtones. However, this teacher trainee related that his students told of how grandfathers sometimes forced their granddaughters to have sex with them. Once again the implications for HIV infection is obvious, while at the same time constituting a heinous crime against children. As reported earlier, children frequently feel uncomfortable reporting sexual abuse at the hands of family members to parents both for cultural reasons and because they will not be believed and will be punished by parents.

Adaptation: the possibilities of critical, culturally-sensitive AIDS education

Mbozi (2000) summarises many of these cultural practices we have discussed according to three categories: (1) social *conduct* resulting from the belief in the powers of an external force, for example ritual cleansing and some dietary taboos; (2) social or sexual *traditions and practices* which are an outgrowth of beliefs related to a perceived role in a social relationship, for example polygamy and circumcision rituals; and (3) social *relations* based on tradition which dictates that something has to be done in a particular way simply because it has been done like that for years, for example wife inheritance and taboos on talking about sex.

This paper contributes to the discussion by providing evidence of the way in which teacher educators and teachers participating in initial or further education identified various cultural practices as 'deceptive' (or *mila potofu*) and made clear how each of these practices sabotaged their efforts at providing effective HIV/AIDS education in their classrooms. Consequently, this final section asks to what extent educators are able to suggest solutions for the existence of *mila potofu* and how these cultural practices might be addressed within educational contexts. Solutions were not immediately apparent. Some reflected on how the most obvious answer, that of directly refuting these beliefs, was also the most short-sighted. Bayer (1994) has repeatedly warned, and empirically illustrated, that:

> AIDS prevention efforts that are not culturally sensitive will be ineffective. They will fail to promote, support, and sustain the behavioural modifications that are the sine qua non of AIDS prevention. They will fail because they will not reach their intended audience, will not be understood by those who are reached, and will not be accepted by those who understand. They may, indeed, provoke outright opposition. (p. 895)

Many educators recognised multiple dilemmas in minimising the harm of *mila potofu*. Teacher trainees reported that parents were against teaching sex education in schools since they claimed it made their children 'immoral'. They were also scared of breaking ingrained cultural taboos regarding adults speaking to children about sex. As a result, schools had to treat sexual content with caution and in some cases it was dropped altogether. Furthermore, as we have already described, there is silence from children, opposition from parents, reluctance from college tutors and embarrassment from female teachers who walk out of rooms when sexual matters are discussed. If the direct topic of deceptive cultural practices is added to the mix, the expected outcome can hardly be positive. However, educators noted that in the face of increasing levels of HIV infection, we simply 'cannot do nothing' or perpetuate the status quo (Bayer, 1994).

In discussion with educators, it become clear that the challenge in the context of sexuality and moral education must be to raise the critical consciousness of students, while allowing them to maintain the integrity of deeply-held cultural beliefs. Otherwise, impositions from above can cause humiliation and provoke resistance that would be counterproductive to the goals of HIV/AIDS education. Educators recommended that 'safe spaces' be created for discussion of sensitive issues that require a highly trained, open-minded, *insider* approach. An open-minded insider to local culture is possibly best placed to conduct critical thinking discussions that draw on human rights discourses, while at the same time discussing ways in which respectful alternatives might be offered. An insider might help students to discuss the values that underpin various cultural practices and find alternative practices without sacrificing the intention behind the practice or custom.

Piaget (1970) describes this as creating a state of disequilibrium, an uncomfortable state that encourages learning and change. Piaget also describes a continuum of three stages along which change occurs when faced with competing values or clashing worldviews. These are 'assimilation', 'accommodation' and 'adaptation'. Using the open-minded critical insider to guide dialogue and reflection among communities regarding *mila potofu,* assimilation of new practices may occur. For Piaget (1970), 'assimilation is the integration of external elements into evolving or completed structures' (p. 706). In this way, a person tries to understand new knowledge in terms of their existing knowledge. Assimilation can further lead to accommodation over time. Piaget defines accommodation as the 'modification of...[a] scheme or structure by the elements it assimilates' (p. 708). The person changes his or her cognitive structure in an attempt to understand new information, adapting his or her way of thinking to a new experience. He adds:

Whereas assimilation is necessary in that it assures the continuity of structures and the integration of new elements to these structures; accommodation...permits structural change. Thus, when taken together, assimilation and accommodation make up adaptation, which refers to the person's ability to adapt to his or her environment. (p. 708)

Disequilibrium thus facilitates 'a need to know', where a person is either motivated to change (a learning) or to work harder to find evidence to confirm his/her belief (a rejection) (Hedgepeth & Helmich, 1996). Our data reveal examples of both sides of disequilibrium. Educators were extremely keen for discussions that interrogated these deceptive cultural practices and suggested culturally sensitive ways to change them by assimilating new practices that might begin to neutralise their effects. For example, in the case of wife inheritance it was suggested that discreet and confidential testing form part of the practice, so that each partner may be informed of the other's serostatus and take the necessary precautions. In fact, many of the cleansing rituals could involve HIV-testing prior to the ceremonies and the use of condoms during it. Another example is the 'medicalisation' of circumcision rituals, with educators suggesting that young men be circumcised in sterile surroundings before going to the bush or mountain for traditional teaching in isolation. Male circumcision in hospitals has already been assimilated in many cultures (Brown *et al.*, 2001; Scott *et al.*, 2005; Bailey *et al.*, 2008). Regarding female circumcision, it was suggested that girls undergo the theoretical sex education that normally accompanied female circumcision but no longer undergo the physical cutting. They would then graduate with paper certificates and relevant knowledge and life skills regarding womanhood. These are good examples from this study on assimilation and adaption, where the harmful cultural practice is not 'attacked' but negotiated resulting in a safer practice. However, there were also some examples of rejection of new information, as evidenced by the teacher's wife who refused to eat eggs despite their nutritional value, the male teacher who supported wife inheritance and the college tutor who resigned himself to teacher trainees 'walking out'. Furthermore, research participants had fewer accommodations to offer with regard to dietary customs and practices grounded in the spirit world.

Conclusion

In the Tanzanian and Kenyan contexts, and in the milieu of HIV/AIDS, cultural practices that might previously have been benign now have dangerous and life-threatening consequences. There have been public outcries over these and other *mila potofu*. However, for as long as we believe education to be an effective 'social vaccine' (Bakilana *et al.*, 2005) and the best option to reach young people, cultural practices should be carefully navigated in order not to estrange community gatekeepers. If these gatekeepers close the door to HIV/AIDS-prevention education, the pandemic has the potential to dramatically worsen.

This paper has offered important examples of the *mila potofu* or deceptive cultural practices, identified by educators in Tanzania and Kenya, which exacerbate the spread of HIV/AIDS and challenge the provision of effective HIV/AIDS education in African classrooms. These educators have identified many of these practices; have begun to reflect on the essence and purposes of these beliefs; and suggest creating safe spaces for insider-led respectful critical thinking and adaptation, while still retaining important cultural values. Human rights education, moral education and HIV/AIDS education delivered by an open-minded critical insider who is both sensitive to cultural practices but who will clearly address those cultural beliefs and practices that impact negatively on the health and well-being of people is critical. To the extent that such an open-minded critical insider helps people to move towards assimilating new values, accommodating new knowledge and adapting (and adopting) new practices, HIV/AIDS prevention may overcome some of the sabotaging cultural practices current in African countries such as Tanzania and Kenya. These are not only moral imperatives but important topics for discussion in moral education classrooms.

Acknowledgements

The authors are grateful to Ingrid van der Heijden and Sharlene Swartz for their detailed comments, which have substantially improved this paper.

References

Ahlberg, B. M. (1994) Is there a distinct African sexuality? A critical response to Caldwell *et al.*, *Africa: Journal of the International African Institute*, 64(2), 220–242.

Ahlberg, B. M., Kimani, V. N., Kirumbi, L. W., Kaara, M. W. & Krantz, I. (1997) Male circumcision: practice and implication for transmission and prevention of STD/HIV in central Kenya, *African Sociological Review*, 1(1), 66–78.

Akinade, A. (2003) Cultural practices that influence the spread of HIV/AIDS in Botswana, in: E. Biakolo, J. Mathangwane & D. Odallo (Eds) *The discourse of HIV/AIDS in Africa* (Pretoria, UNAIDS ICT), 112–116.

Ayikukwei, R., Ngare, D., Sidle, J., Ayuku, D., Baliddawa, J. & Greene, J.Y. (2007) Social and cultural significance of the sexual cleansing ritual and its impact on HIV prevention strategies in western Kenya, *Sexuality and Culture*, 11(3), 32–50.

Bailey, R. C., Egesah, O. & Rosenburg, S. (2008) Male circumcision for HIV prevention: a prospective study of complications in clinical and traditional settings in Bungoma, *Bulletin of the World Health Organization*, 86(9), 669–677.

Bakilana, A., Bundy, D., Brown, J. & Frediksen, B. (2005) *Accelerating the education sector response to HIV/AIDS in Africa: a review of World Bank assistance.* World Bank global HIV/AIDS program discussion paper (Washington DC, World Bank).

Bayer, D. (1994) AIDS prevention and cultural sensitivity, are they compatible? *American Journal of Public Health*, 84(6), 895–898.

Brandt, M. & Rozin, P. (Eds) (1997) *Morality and health* (London, Routledge).

Brown, J. E., Micheni, K. D., Mwenda, J. M., Krchn, D., Muthiri, F. M. & Grant, A. R. (2001) Varieties of male circumcision: a study from Kenya, *Sexually Transmitted Diseases*, 28(10), 608–612.

Bryk, F. (1933) *Voodoo-EROS: ethnological studies in the sex-life of the African Aborigines* (New York, Syd Sculdiner).

Campbell, C. & MacPhail, C. (2002) Peer education, gender and the development of critical consciousness: participatory HIV prevention by South African youth, *Social Science and Medicine*, 55(2), 331–345.

Dilger, H. (2006) The power of AIDS, kinship, mobility and the valuing of social and ritual relationships in Tanzania, *African Journal of AIDS Research*, 5(2), 109–121.

Fine, M. (1988) Sexuality, schooling and adolescent females: the missing discourse of desire, *Harvard Educational Review*, 58(1), 29–53.

Foucault, M. (1976) *The will to knowledge: the history of sexuality* (London, Penguin Books).

Hedgepeth, E. & Helmich, J. (1996) *Teaching about sexuality and HIV: principles and methods for effective education* (New York, New York University Press).

Jeater, D. (1993) *Marriage, perversion and power: the construction of moral discourse in southern Rhodesia 1894–1930* (Oxford, Clarendon Press).

Kelly, R. J., Gray, R. H., Sewankambo, N. K., Serwadda, D., Wabwire-Mangen, F., Lutalo, T. & Wawer, M. J. (2003) Age differences in sexual partners and risk of HIV-1 infection in rural Uganda, *Journal of Acquired Immune Deficiency Syndromes*, 32(4), 446–451.

Kenya Demographic and Health Survey (2003) *Kenya demographic and health survey* (Nairobi, Kenya, Bureau of Statistics).

Kenyatta, J. (1938) *Facing Mount Kenya* (London, Secker & Warburg).

Kiragu, S. W. (2007) Exploring sexuality education and the burdened teacher: a participatory approach in a rural primary school in Kenya, *Pastoral Care in Education*, 25(3), 5–15.

Kiragu, S. W. (2009) *Exploring young people's sexuality in a poor community in Kenya: a case study*, doctoral thesis, University of Cambridge.

Kleinman, A. (1999) Moral experience and ethical reflection, can ethnography reconcile them? A quandary for the 'The New Bioethics', *Daedalus*, 128(4), 69–99.

Leclerc-Madlala, S. (2002) On the virgin cleansing myth: gendered bodies, AIDS and ethnomedicine, *African Journal of AIDS Research*, 1(2), 87–95.

Luginaah I., Elkins D., Maticka-Tyndale E., Landry, T. & Mathui, M. (2005) Challenges of a pandemic: HIV/AIDS-related problems affecting Kenyan widows, *Social Science & Medicine*, 60(6), 1219–1228.

Luke, N. (2002) Widows and 'professional inheritors', understanding AIDS risk perceptions in Kenya. Paper presented at the *Population Association of America Annual Meeting*, Atlanta, GA, 8–11 May.

MacDonald, D. (1996) Notes on the socio-economic and cultural factors influencing the transmission of HIV in Botswana, *Social Science and Medicine*, 42(9), 1325–1333.

Mbozi, P. (2000) The impact of negative cultural practices on the spread of HIV/AIDS in Zambia, in: S. T. K. Boafo & C. A. Arnaldo (Eds) *Media & HIV/AIDS in East and Southern Africa: a resource book* (Paris, UNESCO), 75–82.

Morrell, R. (2003) Silence, sexuality and HIV/AIDS in South African schools, in: B. Tersbøl (Ed.) *Gender, sexuality and HIV/AIDS: research and intervention in Africa.* Proceedings from a seminar held in April, University of Copenhagen.

Mulama, J. (2010, February 23) Turning over a new leaf, *The Daily Nation.* Available online at: http://www.nation.co.ke/magazines/Living/-/1218/867276/-/qb35f12/-/index.html (accessed 25 February 2010).

Oshi, D., Nakalema, S. & Oshi, L. (2005) Cultural and social aspects of HIV/AIDS sex education in secondary schools in Nigeria, *Journal of Biosocial Science*, 37(2), 175–183.

Parker, R. G., Easton, D. & Klein, C. H. (2000) Structural barriers and facilitators in HIV prevention: a review of international research, *AIDS*, 14(1), S22–S32.

Piaget, J. (1970) Piaget's theory, in: P. H. Mussen (Ed.) *Carmichael's manual of child psychology* (vol. 1, 3rd edn) (New York, Wiley).

Scott, B. E., Weiss, H. A., & Viljoen, J. I. (2005) The acceptability of male circumcision as an HIV intervention among a rural Zulu population, KwaZulu-Natal, South Africa, *AIDS Care*, 17(3), 304–313.

Sithole, J. (2003) Cultural factors in the spread and management of HIV/AIDS in Southern Africa, in: E. Biakolo, J. Mathangwane & D. Odallo (Eds) *The discourse of HIV/AIDS in Africa* (Pretoria, South Africa, UNAIDS ICT), 142–144.

UNAIDS (2009) *Fact sheet: sub-Saharan Africa latest epidemiological trends* (Geneva, Switzerland, UNAIDS).

REVIEW ARTICLE

Recent work in African ethics

African ethics: an anthology of comparative and applied ethics
Munyaradzi Felix Murove (Ed.), 2009
Pietermaritzburg, South Africa, University of KwaZulu-Natal Press

Persons in community: African ethics in a global culture
Ronald Nicolson (Ed.), 2008
Pietermaritzburg, South Africa, University of KwaZulu-Natal Press

In this article I review the two books published in the last few years that would be of most interest to those researching or teaching African morality.[1] They are *African ethics: an anthology of comparative and applied ethics* and *Persons in community: African ethics in a global culture*, which are both collections of contemporary essays.[2] These texts are among the first anthologies ever to appear that are strictly devoted to the values of black peoples below the Sahara, and they include many fresh materials that I suggest will be useful to anyone studying comparative ethical systems or the nature of morality.

The literature is replete with anthologies of general African philosophy, which invariably include a handful of papers that address pre-colonial views on ethics. Representative here is *The African philosophy reader* (Coetzee & Roux, 2003), which includes six chapters squarely on morality (and a few more related ones on justice and globalisation), including widely read essays such as 'Person and community in African thought' by Kwame Gyekye and 'The moral foundations of an African culture' by Kwasi Wiredu, the renowned Ghanaian scholars. In contrast, I am aware of only one previously existing collection composed solely of sub-Saharan moral theory (Iroegbu & Echekwube, 2005), which features writings mainly from Nigerian academics, including two dozen contributions by the editors. The two new anthologies are welcome additions to the field, as they address sub-Saharan ethics alone and include many papers that are either new or less widely read and that have been written largely (but not exclusively) by those based in southern Africa.

In what follows I critically discuss not only the editorial choices of which papers to include in these anthologies, but also some of the more striking claims made by the authors of these papers. My aims are both to give the reader a sense of what these books are like and to note some issues raised by these books that warrant more reflection, having implications for the theory and practice of moral education in Africa and wider contexts.

African ethics

African ethics is edited by Munyaradzi Felix Murove, a Zimbabwean who lectures in ethics at the University of KwaZulu-Natal in South Africa. Many of its contributions have been written by those residing in South Africa, with prominent exceptions being 'Africa's wisdom has two parents and one guardian' by Ali Mazrui, the pan-African social theorist and political analyst born in Kenya, and three chapters by Bénézet Bujo, a Congolese theologian and philosopher based in Germany (whom I discuss below). Although the anthology does not include any texts by Ghanaians, Nigerians or other West Africans, it may be fairly taken as a way to highlight important ideas and texts from other parts of the continent that have received less attention. Pairing this book up with, say, the papers on morality in *The African philosophy reader* (Coetzee & Roux, 2003) would give the initially uninformed scholar a solid entry into sub-Saharan ethics from the past two decades.

Murove's aim in putting this collection together is to provide a corrective to Western approaches to ethics, which dominate instruction in many African universities, not to mention those in many other parts of the world. His goal is to present an accessible, convenient forum in which intellectuals from Africa reflect on the values of pre-colonial sub-Saharan peoples in a way that has relevance for global discussions among moral philosophers, professional ethicists, social scientists and educated laypeople. I believe that Murove has clearly realised his goal.

However, I lack the space to demonstrate this conclusively, as the book is so large, having seven parts composed of 24 chapters, thereby giving the reader more than four times what one normally finds on morality in general anthologies. The contributions raise far too many issues to cover in this review, including those in intellectual history (Part 1), ethical theory (Part 2), religion and ethics (Part 3), bioethics (Part 4), business ethics (Part 5), environmental ethics (Part 6) and political justice (Part 7). To obtain focus in a way that minimises overlap with my discussion of *Persons in community* (where bioethics and business ethics figure prominently) and with articles elsewhere in the special issue of this journal (that directly take up ethical theory), below I critically discuss only two substantive topics from *African ethics*, namely, environmentalism and politics.

Several of the papers in *African ethics* are usefully comparative in relating a certain African moral perspective to a Western one and most often contrasting them. Sometimes this is at the level of general principle, with contrasts being drawn between a strand of sub-Saharan ethical philosophy, on the one hand, and Kantian, utilitarian, egoist, discourse or Christian moral theories, on the other. For instance, several chapters emphasise the notion that relationality, community, interconnectedness and spirituality are much more salient in traditional African morality than in contemporary Western ethical thought. At other times, differences are noted at the level of particular judgement, for example 'Does African "corruption" exist?' by

William De Maria suggests that what a typical Westerner deems to be corrupt in politics might differ from what an African does, while '"I am because we are": giving primacy to African indigenous values in HIV/AIDS prevention' by Musa Dube claims that the alleged individual right to confidentiality in medicine conflicts with an African disposition to see illness as a communal affair. Such comparative analysis should be revealing for researchers, instructors and students as they come to grips with sub-Saharan perspectives on morality.

Environmental ethics

With regard to environmentalism, there is a dominant theme present in the chapters by Bujo, Murove and Mogobe Ramose, a South African philosopher whose contribution is a selection from his important book on '*Ubuntu*', the Nguni term for humanness used by many southern Africans to capture morality (Ramose, 1999). The main, common thread is that the basic obligation of *Ubuntu*, to live a genuinely human way of life by living communally with other persons, entails a duty to respect the natural world. This is so for two major reasons that may be distinguished.

First, as Bujo and Ramose emphasise, African worldviews characteristically maintain that all beings in the universe are interrelated to such an extent that the flourishing of one is a function of the flourishing of others. All beings are thought to be not merely connected, but also interdependent with one another. If one's fundamental duty is to help other human beings and if, as a metaphysical or even merely empirical fact, their welfare depends on protecting the natural environment, then one would be wrong to degrade nature.

Second, Murove points out that *Ubuntu*, as traditionally interpreted, requires living communally not merely with existing human beings, but also with past and future generations. With regard to the past, many Africans believe that one has an obligation to live harmoniously with ancestors (the so-called 'living-dead'), who have departed this world but live on in a spiritual realm that is intimately connected with ours. Living harmoniously or communally with ancestors can require behaviour such as protecting land that they are deemed ultimately to own or respecting animals that are ancestral totems. With regard to the future, the present generation of human beings would obviously be failing to live communally with future human beings if it used up natural resources for itself, failing to leave enough and as good for others.

Both rationales contrast with what the authors take to be the dominant Western approach to the environment, which is mechanistic instead of spiritual, and which implies separateness from nature instead of interdependence with it. Even if there are these differences, however, I note that there is also a deep commonality between the sort of environmentalism prominent in *African ethics* and a typically Western approach to the environment: anthropocentrism. Both views largely conceive of natural objects as having value ultimately insofar as they satisfy the interests of persons. However, it is increasingly common among intellectuals, in both parts of the world (e.g. Oruka & Juma, 1994; Brennan & Lo, 2008), to think that many facets of non-human nature have a final value apart from their relation to our well-being. Is there something in African morality that could underwrite a non-anthropocentric approach to the natural world?

One idea that Bujo mentions is that all beings have some worth by virtue of exhibiting a degree of life-force that has come from God. It is thought that there is a ranking of beings in terms of the extent to which they possess a divine energy, with persons at the top, animals coming next, plants after them and then minerals. Such a view entails that everything in nature has a value in itself, meaning that humans are obligated to respect all natural objects, but should, nonetheless, by and large accord themselves a privileged status—an attractive perspective. In future research, it would be worth critically exploring the promise of this view, which relies on a highly contested supernaturalism, as well as probing African moral thought for additional—and perhaps more secular and widely appealing—non-anthropocentric ideas, such as the notion of having a duty to respect purely physical beings in accordance with their capacity for vitality or a duty to treat parts of nature as though they were members of a family.

Politics and democracy

Turning to the chapters on politics in *African ethics*, one also finds a major theme running through many of them, namely, a focus on consensus as essential to just decision-making (setting aside the recurrent discussion of economic justice that one also finds in this part of the book). Invariably, the contributions addressing the questions of who should have political power and of how they should exercise it, by Bujo, Ramose, Augustine Shutte and myself, advocate democracy in lieu of dictatorship but reject the competitive, multi-party style of it one finds without exception in the West. Westerners are used to thinking of democracy in terms of an adversarial contest between political parties, but the contributions to the present volume belie the notion that such a majoritarian system exhausts the attractive options of a modern democratic polity. They all recommend a kind of democratic decision-making that is consensual, seeking unanimity of various kinds on at least all major decisions affecting citizens.

In 'Springboards for modern African constitutions and development in African cultural traditions' Bujo urges contemporary African societies to devise political structures that would better fit their own value systems. Particularly inspired by some traditional practices of a people in Burundi, Bujo notes how it was routine for policy to be determined not unilaterally by a king, but rather by a group of elders who had been popularly appointed and who sought to resolve conflicts in a way that was to the benefit of everyone. Similarly, in 'Towards emancipative politics in modern Africa', Ramose points out that it was common among many indigenous sub-Saharan peoples to seek to resolve conflicts of interest by hearing the views of any adult member of the community and talking until consensus among them was achieved. He maintains that *Ubuntu* fundamentally requires sharing, which includes sharing political power so that decisions are invariably for everyone's sake, not slanted in favour of a majority. Shutte, one of the first professional philosophers in South Africa to engage seriously with African philosophy, argues in his 'Politics and the ethic of *Ubuntu*' that self-realisation through communal relationships means cooperating with everyone in a territory, which, in turn, means that a government should be consultative and encourage grassroots political participation by the people who will be subject to its rules. Finally, in my 'African moral theory and public governance' I contend that in order for a state to avoid promoting discord between it and the rest of society, its officials must not act for the sake of any subset of the population related to them in some way, a principle that not only forbids nepotism and cronyism, but also entails that it is unjust for a politician to act for the sake of a constituency.[3]

The practical objections one might raise to these kinds of schemes are obvious, but the replies given by African political philosophers are worth considering, for example that while consensus among tens of millions of people is unrealistic, it might not be among a small group of their elected representatives. In addition, one can expect objections at the level of principle; some will contend that a consensus-oriented polity would in fact be undemocratic in some way (say, for encouraging a coercive inducement to agree), or might even be too democratic (for precluding a more efficient procedure that would have better social consequences). The point is that real debate is to be had here, and that it is not obvious that the dominant political system in the West—and in Africa, which has copied it—is the just one.

Persons in community

Persons in community is edited by Ronald Nicolson, a retired professor of religious studies at the University of KwaZulu-Natal. The anthology is comprised of seven chapters and a substantial introduction, all of which have been written by people based in southern Africa. The ostensible unifying theme of the book is the search for an African contribution to a 'global ethic', a moral system that (to borrow some language from John Rawls, 1993) could be the object of an 'overlapping consensus' among all or nearly all societies. One might expect, then, that, in contrast to Murove's anthology, the chapters in Nicolson's would mainly highlight the respects in which African morality is similar to that in the West or other ethical traditions. However, disclosing existent common ground is not the general thrust of the contributions to *Persons in community*. Instead, what many of the contributions do is, first, bring out some differences between characteristically African value judgements and others and, second, seek to adjust the value judgements in a way that would make them cohere, thereby helping to *create* a global ethic.

In the rest of this review, I critically discuss the way this strategy is executed in the two contexts of business and medicine in *Persons in community*. This focus means that I cannot address the book's remaining chapters, which seek to reconcile the fundamentals of an *Ubuntu* philosophy with a European, Thomist one (Augustine Shutte), articulate *Ubuntu* morality in light of a spiritual metaphysics (Nhlanhla Mkhize), analyse the relationship between *Ubuntu* and the Truth and Reconciliation

Commission in South Africa (R. Neville Richardson) and discuss the way gendered understandings of *Ubuntu* have a bearing on the HIV/AIDS crisis (Ezra Chitando).

Private business and public administration

In two separate chapters, both Murove and John Mafunisa, a leading scholar of public administration in South Africa, point out that a characteristically Euro-American approach to politico-economic institutions seeks means-ends efficiency. That might be a matter of a business owner treating a worker as part of a machine so as to maximise income and minimise expenditure, as discussed in Murove's 'On African ethics and the appropriation of Western capitalism', or a bureaucracy in which there is a chain of command among civil servants who interact with clients according to inflexible rules, addressed in Mafunisa's 'Ethics, African societal values and the workplace'. Both authors point out that an African morality is incompatible with a thorough-going adherence to what Max Weber (1904/1992) would abbreviate as 'rationalisation' and Jürgen Habermas (1987) would neatly call 'action steered by money and power' (p. 364). African morality, on the face of it, entails a rejection of this form of life that is ubiquitous in the West, since *Ubuntu*'s communal orientation prescribes: cooperating with others and acting for their sake (not competing with others so as to amass profit); working in a way that promotes a sense of togetherness (not reducing labour to a serious of discrete, repetitive tasks undertaken in isolation); making decisions in a collective, democratic way (not unilaterally and hierarchically); and giving some moral weight to religious values and traditional norms (not automatically trading them off to maximise economic or political outcomes).

To resolve these tensions, both Murove and Mafunisa recommend Africanising economic and political organisations, respectively. The ethical ideas associated with talk of '*Ubuntu*' (and cognate terms) originated in societies that, roughly, were stateless and ultimately held land in common (or deemed it to be owned by ancestors), apportioning it to particular families as they needed (or as they warranted for respecting ancestral norms). However, neither Murove nor Mafunisa recommends abolishing capitalism and the state, but rather tempering them with communal values. Murove's most concrete suggestion about what a 'domesticated' or 'indigenised' capitalism might involve is one in which firms do not invariably retrench workers for the sake of a more productive and less expensive technology. His other prescriptions are more abstract, exhorting business people not to be solely self-interested and urging Africans to determine capitalism on their own terms. Mafunisa's recommendations about how to Africanise bureaucracy could also be more usefully specific; it is not action-guiding to say merely that the value of collective decision-making must be 'repositioned in the mainstream' or that civil servants 'must not be too judgmental' of traditionalism among clients.

The next stage of reflection would aim to be clearer about policies that institutions could adopt in order to mitigate the excesses of efficient means-ends behaviour. It would also investigate whether institutions could do so without overly compromising the benefits of such behaviour. Mafunisa suggests that it is possible to 'integrate Western managerial logic and African social ideals, rather than seeing them as incompatible opposites' (p. 122).[4] Perhaps. I worry that much social and economic theory suggests that the more traditional, religious, democratic, flexible and gregarious the interaction between people, the less productive they will be at creating economic wealth and attaining political ends. If that is correct, then it follows that the greater the 'Africanisation' of the sort Murove and Mafunisa prescribe, the less chance there is of improving the lot of the economically worst-off in society. Indeed, one might suspect that, in light of the massive extent of poverty in sub-Saharan Africa, *Ubuntu* might, all things considered, prescribe *more* efficient and rationalised political and economic systems, which could better direct resources to the poorest or enhance their capabilities. What the field of African morality needs is thorough, empirically informed consideration of what *Ubuntu* entails for a modern society, which typically means one with not only capitalism and a state, but also science, industrialisation, multiculturalism, formal education and a mass media.[5]

I am inclined to judge similarly other reconciliations between African and non-African perspectives suggested in *Persons in community*; there are provocative ideas that are unsatisfying as they stand, needing and deserving more thorough investigation. For a second example, let us address some suggestions about how to overcome tensions between African and Western medical norms.

Medical practice

Domoka Lucinda Manda, who lectures in the College of Medicine at the University of Malawi, maintains in 'Africa's healing wisdom' that whereas Western medicine characteristically treats illness as a purely physical matter facing the individual considered apart from her social role, African medicine typically treats it as a spiritual issue facing the person considered in her relation to others.[6] A Western-oriented medical professional would naturally conceive of the cause and cure of illness strictly in terms of the physical state of the individual. For instance, sharp pain in a person's lungs could be a matter of cancer having been triggered by, say, tobacco smoke and would be something to treat with surgery and chemotherapy. In contrast, a more African perspective would consider whether conflictual relationships, either with other human beings or with ancestors, have caused the pain or the cancer, say, because of witchcraft performed by an enemy or punishment imposed by an angry elder in the realm of the 'living-dead'. Consequently, it could well prescribe curing the illness by invoking the help of a shaman to mend these broken religious and social relationships.

Much of the prescriptive disagreement about how a medical professional ought to respond to illness turns on disagreement at a descriptive level. That is, if the empirical and metaphysical debate about whether there are spiritual beings and forces, and about whether they are responsible for illness, could be resolved between cultures, then much of the moral dispute about how medicine should be practised would thereby be resolved, conducing toward a global ethic. However, in the absence of consensus among people about these matters, particularly in Africa where many people simultaneously 'live in two worlds' (viz., the traditional African and the modern Western), one is left with the question of how medicine ought to be carried out in the face of worldviews that compete not merely between people, but often within them as well.

According to Manda, such societies ought to favour a 'medical pluralism' that would include a 'dual healthcare system'. The basic idea is that both forms of medicine should be available to people, without treating one or the other as superior, but rather fostering a mutual exchange between adherents to each system. This is an interesting proposal, but it needs to be weighed up against other interpretations of what *Ubuntu* would prescribe.

For instance, suppose it could be (or, indeed, has been) shown that one form of medicine has a much better success rate than the other. Manda is equivocal about the reliability of African medicine, giving two conflicting judgements about a case where an apparently infertile woman conceived after consulting a shaman. Toward the beginning of the paper, Manda says that 'there could be many explanations' (p. 126) of the healing, including coincidence, but toward the end claims that the case 'supports the view that female infertility indicates a major moral transgression that needs to be corrected on a spiritual level by a traditional healer' (p. 135). Now, a single case of correlation is far from enough to establish causation. Suppose that it were proven, after repeated study, that Western medicine with regard to a particular illness was much more reliable than African. Then *Ubuntu*, which requires caring for others' well-being, would seem to entail that a state—particularly one in Africa that faces extreme shortages of skills and resources and cannot afford two medical systems—should offer only the Western treatment, even if a majority of its citizens believe in the powers of traditional healing.

However, there are African thinkers who would maintain that *Ubuntu* would require a state to uphold traditional culture and do what accords with meanings that a majority of people ascribe to illness, even at the expense of their well-being.[7] Here is another thicket in African ethics that needs to be sorted out: how is one to balance the *Ubuntuist* injunctions to share a way of life, on the one hand, and to care for others' quality of life, on the other, when they conflict? Is there anything general to be said on this score, or is case-by-case judgement the only approach available to balancing these facets of community?

Conclusion

The two new anthologies from Murove and Nicolson raise issues that are likely to broaden the horizons of a global audience and that warrant further analysis in various ways. These texts are a useful contribution to the literature, particularly for those unfamiliar with African ethics. Although there is sometimes a tone in them intimating that an idea should be accepted merely because it is African or non-Western, and although what is presented as a Western idea is sometimes not given a fair shake, the contributions to these volumes raise ways of thinking about morality that are worth exploring, in two respects.

First, these texts would be useful if one wanted to teach or conduct research into comparative ethics, that is, to interpret the ethical beliefs of one's own culture in light of those of another. Especially in a globalised world, it makes sense to familiarise oneself and one's students with a body of value judgements that would be taken seriously by nearly a billion people below the Sahara desert. Note that becoming more aware of traditional African ethics is not a project applicable only to those outside Africa. Many sub-Saharan students who have grown up in urban environments are unfamiliar with the basics of the communal way of life in which their grandparents were probably reared, and it is often true that Western perspectives on morality are the focus of university instruction below the Sahara.

The second purpose for which chapters in Murove's and Nicolson's anthologies would be useful is substantive theoretical and applied ethical analysis. Chances are that a broad type of culture that has been long-standing for so many centuries has something to contribute to our philosophical understanding of morality. The recurrent prizing of community that one encounters in discussion of African morality can be reduced to neither a 'justice' nor a 'care' perspective, which have dominated discussion among moral educationists.[8] And, in this review, I have indicated that particularly worth taking seriously are sub-Saharan ideas about the possibility of a non-competitive democratic polity and a type of administrative-economic system that is not so thoroughly determined by the drive for means-ends efficiency. Additional, under-explored values and practices await the careful and inquisitive reader.

Acknowledgements

For comments on an earlier draft, I thank Sharlene Swartz, Pedro Tabensky, Monica Taylor and an anonymous referee for the *Journal of Moral Education*.

Notes

1. Other recent texts worth mentioning include: manuscripts on sub-Saharan political philosophy (Chachine, 2008; Vervliet, 2009); special issues of journals on African ethics (Tabensky, 2008; van Binsbergen, 2008); unpublished doctoral dissertations (e.g. M. O. Eze, 2008; Matolino, 2009); books that are largely ethnographic analyses of certain values of a specific sub-Saharan people (Shamala, 2008; Chukwube, 2009; Kelbessa, 2009); and books on related topics such as Africana philosophy and critical race theory (E. C. Eze, 2008; Gordon, 2008).
2. To disclose a potential conflict of interest, I note that I have contributed a chapter to *African ethics*.
3. These rationales should be compared with the influential view of Kwasi Wiredu (1996, pp. 172–190) that individuals have a moral right to representation in the formulation of every major political decision.
4. For a similar view, see the chapters on business ethics in Murove (2009) by Barbara Nussbaum ('*Ubuntu* and business') and Mvume Dandala ('Cows never die: embracing African cosmology in the process of economic growth').

5. With regards to this topic, a thoughtful and controversial start is Nkondo (2007).
6. See also the chapters on bioethics in Murove (2009) by Munyaradzi Murove ('African bioethics') and Musa Dube ('"I am because we are": giving primacy to African indigenous values in HIV/AIDS prevention').
7. Or at the expense of well-being *in this world*. Many Africans believe in an afterlife, and some would argue that death of one's body is not necessarily an impairment of one's quality of life, particularly if one would become an ancestor in a spiritual realm (perhaps precisely as a result of participation in traditional healing practices).
8. For more on this point, and on the promise of sub-Saharan morality to provide insight into normative ethics, see 'The African ethic of *Ubuntu/Botho*: implications for research on morality' (Metz & Gaie in this issue, pp. 273–290).

References

Brennan, A. & Lo, Y. (2008) Environmental ethics, in: E. Zalta (Ed.) *Stanford encyclopedia of philosophy (Spring 2008 edition)*. Available online at: http://plato.stanford.edu/entries/ethics-environmental/ (accessed 8 April 2010).

Chachine, I. E. (2008) *Community, justice and freedom: liberalism, communitarianism and African contributions to political ethics* (Uppsala, Sweden, Acta Universitatis Upsaliensis).

Chukwube, O. S. (2009) *Renewing the community and fashioning the individual: a study of traditional communal reconciliation among the Igbo* (Saarbrücken, Germany, VDM Verlag).

Coetzee, P. H. & Roux, A. P. J. (Eds) (2003) *The African philosophy reader* (2nd edn) (New York, Routledge).

Eze, E. C. (2008) *On reason: rationality in a world of cultural conflict and racism* (Durham, NC, Duke University Press).

Eze, M. O. (2008) *The historicity of Ubuntu: an African humanism within contemporary South African socio-political discourse*. PhD dissertation, Universität Witten/Herdecke.

Gordon, L. (2008) *An introduction to African philosophy* (Cambridge, Cambridge University Press).

Habermas, J. (1987) *The philosophical discourse of modernity: twelve lectures* (Cambridge, MA, MIT Press).

Iroegbu, P. & Echekwube, A. (Eds) (2005) *Kpim of morality ethics: general, special and professional* (Ibadan, Nigeria, Heinemann Educational Books).

Kelbessa, W. (2009) *Indigenous and modern environmental ethics: a study of the indigenous Oromo environmental ethic and modern issues of environment and development* (Washington, DC, Council for Research in Values & Philosophy).

Matolino, B. (2009) *The concept of person in African political philosophy: an analytical and evaluative study*. PhD dissertation, University of KwaZulu-Natal.

Nkondo, G. M. (2007) Ubuntu as a public policy in South Africa: a conceptual framework, *International Journal of African Renaissance Studies*, 2(1), 88–100.

Oruka, H. O. & Juma, C. (1994) Ecophilosophy and parental earth ethics, in: H. O. Oruka (Ed.) *Philosophy, humanity and ecology* (Nairobi, ACTS Press), 115–129.

Ramose, M. (1999) *African philosophy through Ubuntu* (Harare, Zimbabwe, Mond Books).

Rawls, J. (1993) *Political liberalism* (New York, Columbia University Press).

Shamala, L. (2008) *The practice of obuntu among the Abaluyia of Western Kenya: a paradigm for community building* (Saarbrücken, Germany, VDM Verlag).

Tabensky, P. (Ed.) (2008) Special issue: African philosophy, *South African Journal of Philosophy*, 27(4), 281–435.

van Binsbergen, W. (Ed.) (2008) Special issue: African philosophy and the negotiation of practical dilemmas of individual and collective life, *Quest: An African Journal of Philosophy/Revue Africaine de Philosophie*, 22(1–2), 2–260.

Vervliet, C. (2009) *The human person: African Ubuntu and the dialogue of civilisations* (London, Adonis & Abbey).

Weber, M. (1904/1992) *The Protestant ethic and the spirit of capitalism* (T. Parsons, Trans.) (London, Routledge).

Wiredu, K. (1996) *Cultural universals and particulars: an African perspective* (Bloomington, IN, Indiana University Press).

REVIEW ARTICLE

The moral tensions of HIV/AIDS in sub-Saharan Africa

The moral economy of AIDS in South Africa
Nicoli Nattrass, 2003
Cambridge, Cambridge University Press

Mortal combat: AIDS denialism and the struggle for antiretrovirals in South Africa
Nicoli Nattrass, 2007
Pietermaritzburg, South Africa, University of KwaZulu Natal Press

The concept of *Botho* and HIV/AIDS in Botswana
Joseph B.R. Gaie and Sana Koketso Mmolai (Eds), 2007
Eldoret, Kenya, Zapf Chancery

Three-letter plague: a young man's journey through a great epidemic
Jonny Steinberg, 2008
Cape Town, South Africa, Jonathan Ball

This article reviews four recent (post-2003) books written by authors living and working in Africa which explore the connection between morality and the HIV epidemic.[1] The books are written from differing perspectives, make use of diverse methodological approaches and present varying conclusions and recommendations. While each work provides considerable scope for discussion in and of itself, this review article attempts to pull the works together by focusing on two major themes that run across all four books and that are critical to developing conversations around morality and HIV, particularly in the sub-Saharan African context. The first of these themes is the intersection between societal and individual morality, while the second is the moral implications of the convergence between scientific method, indigenous knowledge and cultural practice, with respect to human health and well-being.

Moral values, broadly defined as 'principles and fundamental convictions which act as general guides to behaviour, the standards by which particular actions are judged to be good or desirable' (Halstead & Taylor, 2000, p. 175) and which 'provide us with reasons for action' (Halstead & Taylor, 1996, p. 69), are fundamental to understanding the HIV epidemic. In part this is because HIV has historically been understood as a disease of the immoral, related to promiscuity, homosexuality, prostitution and drug abuse (Levy et al., 2005). Even as these prejudices were gradually but not entirely dispelled, AIDS continued to throw up moral issues relating to health and human rights, as highlighted in the work of Jonathan Mann (Mann, 1995; Mann & Tarantola, 1998). For example, early responses to the epidemic tended to put the rights of a healthy public against the rights of HIV-positive individuals, resulting in coercive and restrictive approaches to the disease. Additionally, the close relationships between the spread of HIV and contexts of poverty, oppression, urban migration, gender inequality and social violence highlighted the extent to which social justice could play a key role in prevention (Ligon-Borden, 2003; Fee & Parry, 2008).

Despite Mann's legacy in linking public health and human rights, many moral questions around HIV, individual rights, equality and governance remain insufficiently studied and continue to grow in importance as the epidemic matures. For example, to what extent should governments be obliged to provide high-cost treatment and care to those struggling with chronic and eventually terminal disease? And should policy on AIDS treatment be any different from policy on treatment, for example, for degenerative neuromuscular conditions? In sub-Saharan Africa, as well as parts of Asia, where HIV prevalence is particularly high, resource levels are particularly low and competing needs abound, these questions of societal and governmental morality have become politically prominent and of fundamental moral importance. As evidence is assembled about various HIV interventions, it has become clear that there is a critical intersection between morality at the level of societal policy and practice and morality at the level of individuals. The policies a government makes and the decisions a society takes around AIDS influence the HIV-related beliefs and behaviours of individuals. This in turn, affects levels of transmission as well as the extent to which HIV infection is able to damage a nation's social fabric through, for example, stigma and prejudice.

Economics, AIDS and morality

Two recent books by Nicoli Nattrass, an economist at the University of Cape Town, provide a thorough analysis of arguments for and against public HIV interventions in South Africa, as well as a detailed historical examination of the highly contested, and very gradual roll-out of interventions, including the use of anti-retroviral drugs (ARVs). The first of these books, *The moral economy of AIDS in South Africa*, is primarily economic in nature. However, Nattrass bases her economic analyses on the argument that AIDS cuts 'to the heart of what it means to be a society' (p. 14). It requires us to assess what level of responsibility the state—and by extension, fellow-citizens, or members of a national moral community—holds to those who are infected by HIV.

For many years, the South African government, and most notably former president Thabo Mbeki and Health Minister Manto Tshabalala-Msimang, refused to acknowledge that AIDS was a disease caused by the Human Immunodeficiency Virus. On the basis of what is called 'denialism', the claim that HIV does not cause AIDS, ARV-based prevention and treatment for AIDS was not made available in public health services. *The moral economy of AIDS in South Africa* was written in the wake of a legal battle to compel the South African government to provide prevention of mother to child transmission (PMTCT) ARV services. This particular context shapes the book's content and argument.

Although South African public policy has now shifted in favour of ARV roll-out (even if implementation still falls far short of needs) (World Health Organisation, 2008), the book's core moral question, whether individuals have a state-guaranteed right to best available healthcare, remains contemporary. The recent emergence of proposals in South Africa for a national health insurance, and general dissatisfaction with the level of service delivery in the public health sector, suggests that this is an issue which is unlikely to disappear (Ncayiyana, 2009). It is also not an issue limited to South Africa, or indeed the developing world, as is illustrated by recent debate on healthcare reform in the USA.

The moral fight for antiretrovirals

Nattrass's second book, *Mortal combat: AIDS denialism and the struggle for antiretrovirals in South Africa*, grounds her detailed historical analysis of the battle for public access to antiretroviral drugs in the economic analyses of her 2003 book. In it, she attempts to understand the reasons why AIDS denialism had such a substantial and long-lasting impact on South African AIDS policy. The answer provided relates to state structure and political pressures for conformity with the views of those at the highest level of government. The question of how AIDS denialism came to have such strong support at the highest levels of the state is, however, far more challenging and more difficult to answer. In searching for answers, a recurring theme presented by Nattrass is the different ways in which 'Western' and indigenous knowledge are understood and evaluated in the South African context.

Although clearly in favour of widespread government provision of ARVs to those suffering from AIDS, Nattrass stops short of making this an explicit recommendation in her books. Instead, she highlights the important nature of decision making on this topic and the substantial role that civil society actors have already played in enabling a complete turnaround in South Africa's AIDS policies. In a context of deep inequality and limited resources, making decisions on AIDS policy is fundamentally moral in nature. An AIDS policy in which government becomes responsible for universal treatment provision may require the investment—and collection—of additional resources and/or the short- or longer-term renunciation of other policy objectives. Given the extent of the epidemic, and the high economic costs of both action and inaction, public involvement in decision making is crucial to ensuring that the public is willing to bear the costs and consequences of policy. In fact, Nattrass makes a strong argument that for governance to be moral, it must be both consultative and evidence-driven (pp. 188–189). While obviously more complex in practice than in theory, the underlying idea is that the moral responsibility of government therefore lies first in providing its populace with clear and complete information, and perhaps also the skills with which to interpret this information, and only then in developing policy.

Although her focus is firmly on moral behaviour at the societal level, Nattrass (in both books) illustrates the connection between societal and individual moral behaviour by describing the ways in which they influence each other. For example, she provides evidence on how the availability of ARV treatment increases the take-up of voluntary counselling and testing (VCT), while VCT take-up in turn may drive behaviour change, thereby reducing HIV transmission. Similarly, but more broadly, the work is driven in part by the underlying belief that providing individuals with the opportunity to participate in policy formation will result in a citizenry more committed to the implementation of the policy and more willing to put up with any hardships or tradeoffs resulting from policy choices. That is, empowering individuals to participate in societal decision making is likely to result in, over the longer term, behaviours and actions that are more beneficial to society at large—again highlighting the intersection between societal and individual morality.

The significance of empowering individuals to Nattrass' argument for morality also brings out the second theme: the question of how individuals and society should relate to and interpret both indigenous and 'Western', or scientifically generated, knowledge. Nattrass acknowledges that the deep-seated scepticism felt by many South Africans towards 'science' is very closely related to historical experiences of science as a weapon (both physical and cultural), first of colonisers, later of the Apartheid government and now corrupted by industrial interests (see Nattrass, 2008). She also makes very clear that a great deal of scientifically generated and confirmed information, particularly with regards to AIDS, has been created in Africa, and often by African scientists. The tendency to generalise all scientific knowledge as Western is therefore fundamentally flawed. Nattrass could, however, perhaps have gone a little further in exploring the idea that there is, in fact, no fundamental conflict between scientific method and indigenous knowledge. There is no reason not to evaluate indigenous knowledge in a way that is both scientific and accepted and, indeed, to use this to ensure that the most useful elements of indigenous knowledge are protected, developed and used, rather than discarded.

Nattrass illustrates how the confusion between genuine indigenous knowledge, worthy of exploration, and discredited ideas of unclear provenance, appears to have been central to the catastrophic policy decisions made by the South African government. By putting these two different types of ideas—the indigenous and the discredited—on a common footing, denialism has provided the impression of a fundamental conflict between genuine science and indigenous knowledge. This has been harmful and, indeed, fatal. Not only have lives been lost and the general credibility of indigenous beliefs been challenged without real reason, but many people have also been deprived of their fundamental democratic rights to participate in decision making.

While Nattrass' work is fundamentally scientific—some might say 'Western'—in nature, this appears to have had the effect of pushing her to argue for providing African people with far more authority and autonomy than is supported by many of the purveyors of indigenous knowledge and medicine. She argues that citizens should be empowered to shape societal decision making. By contrast, some proponents of allegedly indigenous or traditional African knowledge or behaviour appear to condone the disempowerment of ordinary African people by stripping them of various human rights. Examples include recent actions against homosexuals in Uganda or the imposition of extreme forms of Sharia law in northern Nigeria, both of which are argued to be based on indigenous beliefs but which have damaged individuals' rights to freedom from discrimination and limited their decision-making agency.

African culture and HIV/AIDS

Botho, along with *Ubuntu* (see Metz and Gaie, pp. 273–290, and Ramose, pp. 291–303 in this issue), is defined as a way of being genuinely human that depends fundamentally on 'moral' relationships with other humans (Gaie, 2007a, p. 29). *Botho*, by stressing the interconnectedness of people in a community, implies that the illness of one affects all, making HIV a community-wide affair. Despite this definition, rather than looking at issues of societal or community-wide morality, *The concept of Botho and HIV/AIDS in Botswana* focuses very much on the behaviour of individuals and when this is and is not judged to be moral. The result is that Gaie and Mmolai's recommendations largely ignore public health interventions in favour of individual-level interventions, generally focused on identifying infected individuals and preventing further spread. Given that the book is focused on morality as defined by *Botho*, the silence on supportive interventions for those affected or infected by HIV, such as PMTCT and ARV treatment, is puzzling. In fact, some chapters are written as though medical management of HIV were impossible, even as Botswana is in the process of rolling out the most substantial prevention and treatment programme in sub-Saharan Africa (WHO, UNAIDS & UNICEF, 2008).

Examples of policy recommendations in the volume that focus on controlling individuals include mandatory HIV testing and disclosure of results for all 'maids' (Botshelo, 2007, p. 57), and students receiving funding for foreign study (Gaie, 2007b, p. 119). Strong arguments are also made for replacing condom provision with abstinence-only programmes (Mmolai, 2007, p. 74–75), even though the limitations of this approach have been well documented (Blum, 2004; Setswe, 2007). These recommendations by Mmolai (2007) are predicated on a need to control individuals and their behaviour, rather than empower them in any way. Additionally, many of the recommendations raise concerns about individual rights and medical confidentiality. The value and validity of these concerns are thorny issues in an epidemic which has been fuelled by silence—stemming from denial of the causes and extent of the disease, ignorance about prevention and treatments and traditional stances on sexual morality and stigma (Levy *et al.*, 2005)—and where community mobilisation has proved critical in developing solutions. While this would make for an interesting discussion and could lend substantial weight to some of the arguments advanced in the volume, it is not pursued.

Another striking absence in the volume is the failure to acknowledge empirical evidence, including the findings of work conducted in Africa, and by Africans, to support or refute arguments. In fact, as argued so forcefully by Nattrass (*The moral economy of AIDS in South Africa, Mortal combat*, 2008), the large majority of this empirical evidence tends to suggest that public health interventions are critical to controlling the spread of HIV and to mitigating its most deleterious effects. Unfortunately, Gaie and Mmolai, in *The concept of Botho and HIV/AIDS in Botswana*, do not explain why they choose not to allow empirical evidence any role in shaping their policy recommendations. This constitutes a missed opportunity for a valuable or at least illuminating discussion. Understanding whether this omission of existing evidence on HIV-related policies is due to a rejection of the scientific approach underlying HIV research, a rejection of the moral assumptions underlying this research or something else entirely would be valuable in providing the reader with the tools to appropriately assess and understand the arguments in this volume.

Finally, it is worth emphasising again that although allegedly guided by the indigenous and traditional concept of *Botho*,[2] rather than by 'Western' science, the recommendations in this volume could disempower Africans and deprive them of their autonomy. This is a strikingly different, and less favourable, outcome, for both individuals and society more broadly, than that advocated by Nattrass (in *The moral economy of AIDS in South Africa* and *Mortal combat*). This highlights just how critical it is that all knowledge, regardless of provenance, receives critical and scientific assessment and is discarded if found wanting.

Moral perceptions of an epidemic

Steinberg's *Three-letter plague*[3] is in many ways the richest of the four books reviewed in terms of getting at the very core of how the HIV epidemic interacts with morality. The book reveals how the HIV/AIDS pandemic has impacted the lives of people living in a rural South African community. Steinberg tells the story of a young man, Sizwe, navigating his way through the AIDS epidemic. As a work of reportage, the book does not provide generalisable conclusions or scientific evidence. What it does, however, is open up discussion around a range of moral and social issues related to AIDS, as well as suggesting to researchers valuable directions in which scientific work might travel. At the core, and never entirely answered, is Steinberg's key question around why so many people continue not to access the various HIV/AIDS services that are gradually being made available.

A partial answer to this question appears to be related, again, to knowledge and information. Indeed, the book is highly informative around the ways in which HIV-related information (and mis-information) has become available to at least the members of one small rural community in South Africa and how this hampers and paralyses their ability to make moral decisions in the context of the epidemic. Interestingly, Steinberg's account echoes at the individual level, the story which Nattrass tells at the societal level, of how South Africans are deprived of access to the information that would enable effective participation in decision making by government. Access to information appears, in fact, to be a core connection between morality in terms of public-sector action and morality at the level of individual behaviour. After all, how can one make a moral decision without access to information that can be trusted?

This brings us again squarely to the theme of the validity of both scientific and indigenous knowledge. *Three-letter plague* vividly illustrates the impacts of suspicion about the goals of 'Western' medicine, as well as a willingness to believe too easily in treatments and 'cures' that are portrayed as indigenous. Concerns about how to interpret information and the meaning of science, as well as indigenous knowledge and traditional beliefs and, in the contemporary era, how to integrate these different bodies of knowledge, are clearly real, present and important——life-threateningly so—in the lives of many South Africans (and in the rest of Africa).

Three-letter plague's focus and strength lie in the way in which it is able to approach morality at the level of the individual. Through this it is able to advance, and justify, an underlying argument that government has a responsibility to provide HIV prevention and treatment services to its populace, along with information, and the tools to assess any other information they encounter. Steinberg provides vivid illustrations of how policy decisions to provide—or withhold—services impact on the lives of individuals and on their subsequent behaviours. Once again, the relationship between governmental and societal decisions and those made by individuals is highlighted.

Steinberg also illustrates the ways in which the intersection between societal and individual-level morality is shaped not just by the existence of policy or the provision of services, but also very much by the nature of their implementation. An example of this is when Sizwe tells Steinberg that people could tell who tested HIV-positive by the length of time they spent in post-test counselling (p. 31). Sizwe even describes how, during a well-advertised testing day, some villagers had gone to the testing centre merely to watch other people getting tested. The tension between disclosure and exposure—something most people are not willing to do—would make it harder for those potentially at risk to test, increasing the chances that they would rather remain ignorant of their status. The extent to which services are difficult to access, or are experienced as sites of conflict or coercion, influences the extent to which they can be successful. This is yet another strong argument for the empowerment and involvement of individuals in making decisions around the development of HIV policy, as well as its implementation.

Conclusion

This review suggests that at least some work emerging from the sub-Saharan Africa context is coming to grips with the concept that both individual and public moral decisions are critical in shaping how the HIV epidemic will continue to unfold. Neither can operate successfully without the other and each is strengthened by the vitality of the other. Empowering individuals to participate in decision making in both spheres appears critical, not just to health and the control of the HIV epidemic, but also to constructing a genuinely democratic society. The central importance of empowering individuals to participate in decision making highlights again the second theme of how to evaluate knowledge and information. While this debate appears to be attracting growing attention, both politically and academically, the works reviewed here tend to suggest that African societies remain far from finding satisfactory ways to assess information. Not only do citizens lack access to reliable and trustworthy information, they also often lack the tools (scientific, analytical and cultural) with which to critically assess the information that they do encounter. This appears to be an area in which moral education could make a valuable contribution.

Notes

1. Although the original intention was to focus only on books published since 2007, we decided to include Nattrass (2003) because it provides historical detail on morality and the state in provision of healthcare in the context of AIDS, as well as forming the empirical and theoretical base on which her subsequent work is founded.
2. Elsewhere in this issue Gaie and Metz, and Ramose, provide deeper and more comprehensive articulations of *Botho/Ubuntu* that are likely to challenge Gaie and Mmolai's views here.
3. Outside South Africa the book was also published under the title: *Sizwe's test: a young man's journey through a great epidemic* (Simon & Schuster).

References

Blum, R. (2004) Uganda AIDS prevention: A, B, C and politics, *Journal of Adolescent Health*, 34(5), 428–432.

Botshelo, I. (2007) The maid, *Botho* and HIV & AIDS infections: the economic and ethical perspectives, in: J. Gaie & S. Mmolai (Eds) *The concept of Botho and HIV/AIDS in Botswana* (Eldoret, Kenya, Zapf Chancery), 45–60.

Fee, E. & Parry, M. (2008) Jonathan Mann, HIV/AIDS and human rights, *Journal of Public Health Policy*, 29(1), 54–71.

Gaie, J. (2007a) The Setswana concept of Botho: unpacking the metaphysical and moral aspects in: J. Gaie & S. Mmolai (Eds) *The concept of Botho and HIV/AIDS in Botswana* (Eldoret, Kenya, Zapf Chancery), 29–43.

Gaie, J. (2007b) Should prospective students be tested for HIV/AIDS prior to overseas scholarship grants? A moral perspective in: J. Gaie & S. Mmolai (Eds) *The concept of Botho and HIV/AIDS in Botswana* (Eldoret, Kenya, Zapf Chancery), 101–126.

Halstead, J. M. & Taylor, M. J. (1996) *Values in education and education in values* (London, Falmer Press).

Halstead, J. M. & Taylor, M. J. (2000) Learning and teaching about values: a review of the literature, *Cambridge Journal of Education*, 30(2), 169–202.

Levy, N., Miksad, R. & Fein, O. (2005) From treatment to prevention: the interplay between HIV/AIDS treatment availability and HIV/AIDS prevention programming in Khayelitsha, South Africa, *Journal of Urban Health*, 82(3), 498–509.

Ligon-Borden, B. (2003) Dr. Jonathan Mann: champion for human rights in the fight against AIDS, *Seminars in Paediatric Infectious Diseases,* 14(4), 314–322.

Mann, J. (1995) Human rights and the new public health, *Health and Human Rights,* 1(3), 229–233.

Mann, J. & Tarantola, D. (1998) Responding to HIV/AIDS: a historical perspective, *Health and Human Rights,* 2(4), 5–8.

Mmolai, S. (2007) Methods used to combat HIV & AIDS in Botswana: implications for *Botho,* in: J. Gaie & S. Mmolai (Eds) *The concept of Botho and HIV/AIDS in Botswana* (Eldoret, Kenya, Zapf Chancery), 71–83.

Nattrass, N. (2008) AIDS and the scientific governance of medicine in post-Apartheid South Africa, *African Affairs,* 107(427), 157–176.

Ncayiyana, D. (2009) NHI or bust—the road of no return to healthcare reform, *South African Medical Journal,* 99(11), 765.

Setswe, G. (2007) Abstinence and faithfulness programmes for prevention of HIV/AIDS among young people: what are the current debates? *South African Family Practice,* 49(8), 5–10.

World Health Organization (WHO), Joint United Nations Programme on HIV/AIDS (UNAIDS) & United Nations Children's Fund (UNICEF) (2008) *Towards universal access: scaling up priority HIV/AIDS interventions in the health sector. Progress report June 2008* (Geneva, Switzerland, WHO).

Index

Page numbers in **Bold** represent figures.

For Product Safety Concerns and Information please contact our EU
representative GPSR@taylorandfrancis.com Taylor & Francis Verlag GmbH,
Kaufingerstraße 24, 80331 München, Germany

Batch number: 08151665

Printed by Printforce, the Netherlands